# DESIGNING AND BUILDING A HORIZONTAL / VERTICAL METAL CUTTING BANDSAW

Written and Illustrated by
Vincent R. Gingery

Introduction by
David J. Gingery

Printed in the U.S.A.

FIRST EDITION

FIRST PRINTING 1995


COPYRIGHT © 1995 VINCENT R. GINGERY

ALL RIGHTS RESERVED


LIBRARY OF CONGRESS
CATALOG CARD NUMBER 95-79289


INTERNATIONAL STANDARD BOOK NUMBER
1-878087-17-7


PUBLISHED BY
DAVID J. GINGERY PUBLISHING
P.O. BOX 75
FORDLAND, MISSOURI 65652-0075

IN MEMORY OF OUR GOOD FRIEND HAROLD BLUMENSTOCK. Harold showed us it could be done. He died shortly before this book went to press. Life just isn't the same without him and we miss him very much.

SPECIAL THANKS TO OUR GOOD FRIEND DON COKLEY. He put up with us for a couple of weeks while we used his shop. It was winter time and his shop was heated. Besides, his lathe is nicer than ours. He also gave us a few pointers on cutting pipe with an oxy-acetylene torch.

## TABLE OF CONTENTS

INTRODUCTION. . . . . . . . . . . . . . . . . . . . . . . . . . . . . . . . . . . . 6

DESIGN CONSIDERATIONS. . . . . . . . . . . . . . . . . . . . . . . . . . 9

CONSTRUCTION METHODS . . . . . . . . . . . . . . . . . . . . . . . . . 17

MATERIAL LIST . . . . . . . . . . . . . . . . . . . . . . . . . . . . . . . . . . 23

DRAWING NOTES . . . . . . . . . . . . . . . . . . . . . . . . . . . . . . . . 32

BUILDING THE BASE . . . . . . . . . . . . . . . . . . . . . . . . . . . . . . 33

BUILDING THE LEGS . . . . . . . . . . . . . . . . . . . . . . . . . . . . . . 36

BUILDING THE LANDING GEAR . . . . . . . . . . . . . . . . . . . . . . 46

BUILDING THE VISE . . . . . . . . . . . . . . . . . . . . . . . . . . . . . . 55

THE VERTICAL FRAME ASSEMBLY . . . . . . . . . . . . . . . . . . . . 65

THE COUNTER SHAFT STAND AND MOTOR MOUNT . . . . . . . . 81

THE DRIVE SHAFT STAND . . . . . . . . . . . . . . . . . . . . . . . . . . 88

THE UPPER VERTICAL FRAME ASSEMBLY . . . . . . . . . . . . . . . 91

# TABLE OF CONTENTS (Continued)

BUILDING THE IDLER WHEEL BEARING ASSEMBLY . . . . . . . . 103

THE IDLER WHEEL FRAME ASSEMBLY . . . . . . . . . . . . . . . . . 106

THE BLADE TENSION ADJUSTMENT ASSEMBLY . . . . . . . . . . 109

THE BELT DRIVE ASSEMBLY . . . . . . . . . . . . . . . . . . . . . . . . 112

DECIDING WHICH PULLEYS TO USE . . . . . . . . . . . . . . . . . . . 113

THE DRIVE SHAFT AND COUNTERSHAFT . . . . . . . . . . . . . . . 114

MOUNTING THE MOTOR . . . . . . . . . . . . . . . . . . . . . . . . . . . . 119

THE BLADE GUIDES . . . . . . . . . . . . . . . . . . . . . . . . . . . . . . . 120

MAKING THE BLADE GUIDE ROLLERS . . . . . . . . . . . . . . . . . .121

MAKING THE ECCENTRIC BOLTS . . . . . . . . . . . . . . . . . . . . . 123

THE LOWER BLADE GUIDE ASSEMBLY . . . . . . . . . . . . . . . . . 123

THE UPPER BLADE GUIDE ASSEMBLY . . . . . . . . . . . . . . . . . 129

MOUNTING THE FEED PRESSURE CONTROL SPRING . . . . . . . 132

MAKING A HANDLE FOR THE VERTICAL FRAME . . . . . . . . . . 136

MAKING THE BLADE COVERS . . . . . . . . . . . . . . . . . . . . . . . 137

MAKING A COVER FOR THE DRIVE SHAFT . . . . . . . . . . . . . . 141

THE AUTOMATIC SHUT OFF ASSEMBLY . . . . . . . . . . . . . . . . 143

MAKING A HANDLE FOR THE SAW TABLE . . . . . . . . . . . . . . 146

A HANDLE FOR THE VISE SCREW SHAFT . . . . . . . . . . . . . . . 148

MAKING THE BLADE WHEELS . . . . . . . . . . . . . . . . . . . . . . . 149

# TABLE OF CONTENTS (Continued)

MOUNTING THE BLADE WHEELS . . . . . . . . . . . . . . . . . . . . . . 160

MOUNTING THE SAW BLADE . . . . . . . . . . . . . . . . . . . . . . . . 161

ADJUSTING THE BLADE . . . . . . . . . . . . . . . . . . . . . . . . . . . . 163

SETTING THE VISE UP FOR MITER CUTS . . . . . . . . . . . . . . . . 166

CUTTING PROBLEMS AND CAUSES . . . . . . . . . . . . . . . . . . . 166

THERE ARE SERIOUS HAZARDS IN THE PROCESSES AND PROCEDURES IN THIS BOOK. NO ATTEMPT HAS BEEN MADE TO POINT OUT ALL OF THE DANGERS OR EVEN A MAJORITY OF THEM. THE METHODS AND MATERIALS THAT ARE SUGGESTED IN THIS MANUAL WERE DEVELOPED BY A NON-PROFESSIONAL. THE AUTHOR IS NOT AN ENGINEER OR SCIENTIST AND NO CLAIM IS MADE TO THE PROPRIETY OF THE METHODS SUGGESTED IN THESE PAGES. THE READER IS FULLY RESPONSIBLE FOR DEVISING SAFE PROCEDURES FOR EVERY OPERATION.

# INTRODUCTION

It is now more than 16 years since the original "METAL SHOP FROM SCRAP" series was conceived. The intention then was to retrace the steps of the pioneers of the industrial revolution and to partially relive the experience of evolving machine tools from such materials as might be easily at hand, available cheaply, and by means that are practical for home construction by amateurs. To my total surprise the series was well received. Many thousands of copies have sold and countless people around the world have built practical machinery at home while learning the basic principles of pattern making, metal casting and metal working by hand and machine. Many people have carried the idea far beyond my vision and some have built machinery of amazing quality. It is evident that far more is possible than has been accomplished to date. And it is unlikely that limits will be found as long as practical people apply themselves to shaping ordinary substance into those articles and devices that enhance the quality of life.

Obviously it required some research to discover the approximate sequence of the development of machinery from about 1740 through 1900. There was never an intent to accurately document the real times and events. But a practical starting point was needed and it was of value to have an idea of how others had progressed through what I intended to do. The logical first step was the foundry since machinery is made of many castings. My shop was devoid of any equipment except a sturdy work bench with a hefty vise. And I had a limited set of hand tools which included a hacksaw and a 3/8" electric hand drill. The objective was to discover whether I could apply my limited equipment and basic hand skills to produce patterns and castings, and progressively work those castings into functioning machines. The premise was that I should be able to learn what others had learned and thus do what they had done. The result was a fully functional machine shop that includes a foundry, a lathe, a shaper, a milling machine, a drill press, tooling and accessories for all of the machines and a sheet metal brake.

The cost was minimal and the labor intense. There is no way I could set a sale price on my shop today. And I suspect that if I priced it to recover material costs and reasonable labor, commercially manufactured equipment might seem cheap by comparison. But far more important and valuable is the knowledge and skill I acquired in the building. My most prized achievement is that I have proven that I can learn what others know and I can acquire the skills I admire in others. Not only that, but I discovered that I could also communicate information to others and inspire them to take up similar activity. And nothing could have pleased me more than when my son chose to carry on when I retired.

Initially the idea of building a band saw was inspired by one I'd seen built by my local friend, Harold Blumentsock. I happen to have a cheap imported band saw that is certainly better than the hand hacksaw I used in building my original shop. But Harold's machine is so superior in quality and capacity that we decided to develop one for home construction and publish a manual. To be sure, if you want a light duty machine that will whack off a length of bar stock you might consider a cheap import. But if you want a hefty, quality machine that will cut large stock quickly and accurately this project is for you. And building it will bring far greater pleasure and satisfaction than merely plunking down a couple hundred bucks.

This band saw project began as a joint effort, but I soon realized that Vince was well able to carry it out without my help or hindrance. We very much enjoyed the initial time as we designed and built the base. But we were simply having too much fun and progress was too slow to suit either of us. We decided that progress was more important than pleasure. I was acutely aware that such work requires continuity and freedom from distraction. And being of an age when deteriorating vision and diminished energy makes me more interested in pursuit of pleasure than achievement, I gleefully retired and dumped it in Vince's lap. I could not be more pleased with the final product. I don't know what would have resulted if we'd continued together. But it would not have been a better machine. Along with a more scholarly approach, Vince brings his superior CAD skills and enthusiasm to produce an excellent project manual that I am extremely proud of.

    David J. Gingery

## DESIGN CONSIDERATIONS

Before you begin this project, there are several things to consider as well as several questions you need to ask yourself. I know because we have thought about building a bandsaw for several years, but there seemed to be many hurdles to over come such as cost, time, and if the project would be worth while. After all, you can buy one of the import saws for less than $200.00. In the beginning, having only limited funds, that's what we did; we bought a cheap saw. All things considered, the saw was okay for light duty use, but it wasn't long before we discovered a few problems with it. We couldn't complain very loudly though. After all, you get what you pay for.

One of the things encountered on our import saw, was a flimsy stand which caused the saw to be easily knocked over. Another problem was the length of time it took to cut larger pieces of material. It was also difficult to keep the blade adjusted for a straight cut. The 1/2" blades were easy to break, and the blade was prone to slip when under a load. It was not unusual for the blade to come completely off the wheel. The blade wheels did not allow clearance for the teeth on the saw blade. This caused the teeth on the blade to flatten against the wheel and loose their set. Blade set means the bending of the teeth to the right and left to allow clearance so that the blade back can follow through the cut. When the set is flattened the blade binds, and overheats causing it to dull or break.

It wasn't long before we were forced to make a choice. Either modify and rebuild our cheap import saw, or forget it completely and design and build our own. We remembered that our friend Harold Blumenstock had built a saw several years ago. We decided to ask him if we could have a look at it. Harold was happy to show it to us. A picture of his saw is shown in fig. 1. It was built in 1968 and this photo was taken in 1994. As you can see the saw has held up very well and is still in good working order.

Listening to Harold describe and demonstrate his saw gave us many ideas for building our own. But most of all he showed us that it could be done.

As you can see in fig. 1, Harold's saw was built from angle iron, flat bar and 1/4" steel plate.

**Figure 1**  Harold Bloomenstock's horizontal bandsaw.

The blade wheels are made from 12" pipe with a hub held in the center by spokes. The blade wheels were turned on a lathe. The worm gear drive was taken from an old Maytag washing machine. The spring on the back keeps the saw blade from coming down too hard on the work. The vise handle was taken from an old water main valve.

As we began designing our own bandsaw we decided we would like to be able to use our saw in a vertical position, as well as the horizontal position. We also found that coming up with a worm gear drive from an old maytag washer was no easy task and the price of a new gear box was more than we could afford.

These considerations as well as others caused us to make our saw somewhat different than Harold's. As my Dad would say,

**Figure 2**  Dave Gingery on the left and Harold Bloomenstock on the Right discussing the construction of a bandsaw.

the best way to describe the design of our saw is that it is a conglomeration of all the ideas we ever got from every saw we ever saw.

Drawings of our bandsaw design are shown in fig. 3 and 4, and a photo representation is shown in fig. 5. The maximum work piece width capacity of our saw is 12". The throat depth is 6". From the drawings you can see that the saw frame is constructed entirely of easy to find angle and flat bar. With the exception of the leg braces, the vertical post brace and the table ends, which are welded, most assembly is done with nuts and bolts of varying sizes.

The saw table is 36" long and 9" wide. The top is made from 1/4 x 3 x 4 angle. The top is held together by a 1/4 X 3 x 8-1/2 plate which is welded at each end. The top is built with a 2" wide opening for the vise travel nut. The opening runs down the length of the table and is offset to the right which causes the main clamping force of the vise to be closer to the saw blade.

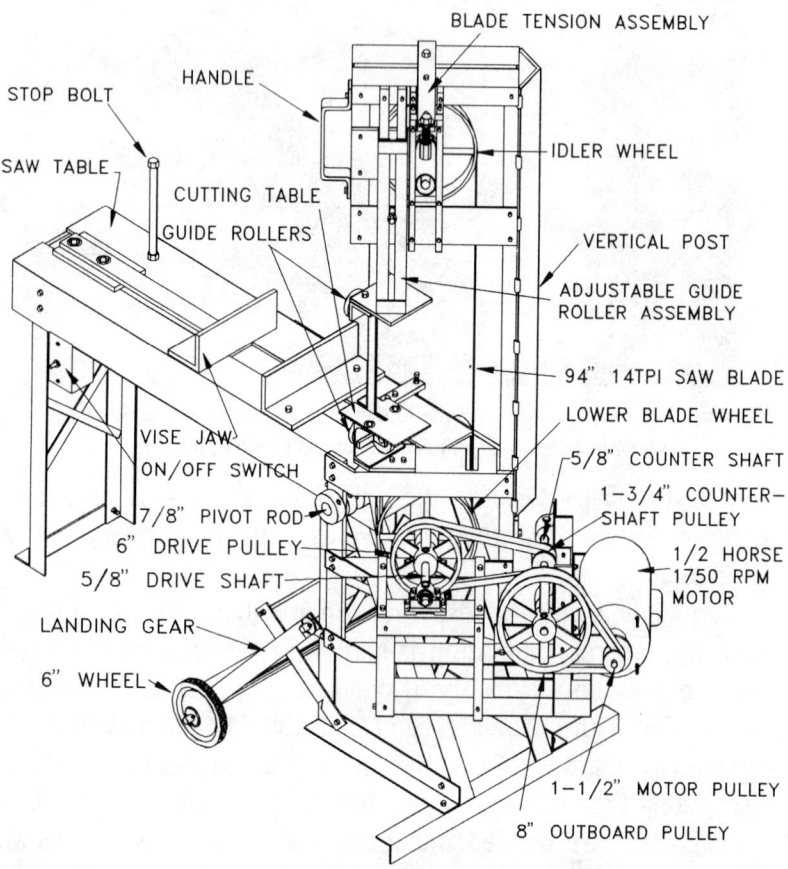

**Figure 3**  Right side view of the horizontal/vertical bandsaw

    The front, middle and rear legs are made from 1-1/2" angle. They hold the table 24" off the ground. Each pair of legs are cross braced with 3/4" strap iron welded between them.
    The wheel assembly pivots on a hinge mounted to the middle legs. The wheels are 6" metal hub lawn mower wheels.

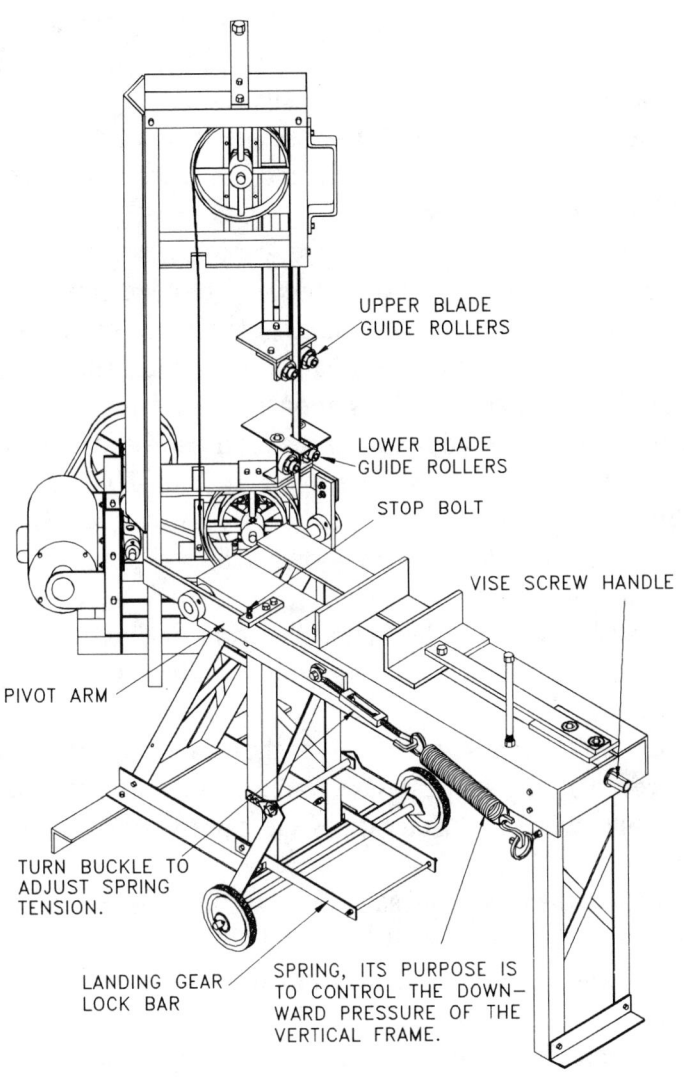

**Figure 4**     Left side view of bandsaw

The wheel assembly is engaged by raising the front of the saw causing the wheel assembly to drop down. Notches in the lock bar lock on the cross brace of the wheel frame and prevent the wheel frame from moving. With the wheels in the locked position the machine can be moved easily.

To release the wheel assembly, raise the front of the table, release the lock bar, lower the table and the wheels will drop out of position stabilizing the saw.

The purpose of the vise is to hold the workpiece secure as the saw makes its cut. It consists of a threaded rod and travel nut that moves the vise clamp jaw either forward or backward, depending on which way the screw handle is turned. The clamp jaw holds the work against the stationary jaw. If desired the stationary jaw can be adjusted so material can be cut off at different angles. The vise jaws are made of 3/8 x 3 x 3 angle.

The vertical saw frame is bolted to pivot arms located on each side of the saw. The arms pivot on a 7/8" rod enabling the saw to cut in a horizontal position.

The adjustable stop bolt located at the front of the saw table determines how far the saw will drop into the horizontal cutting position.

The stop bolt located at the rear of the saw table shown in fig. 4 prevents the vertical saw frame from falling too far back. In other words, it determines the saws vertical cutting position.

The blade wheel on the saw is powered through pulley reduction by a 1/2 HP, 1750 RPM, 120 volt electric motor.

A 1-1/2" pulley is mounted on the shaft of the motor. A "V" belt connects the motor pulley to the 8" outboard pulley on the counter shaft. This reduces the counter shaft speed to 282.25 RPM. Another "V" belt connects a 1-3/4 pulley on the center of the counter shaft with a 6" pulley on the drive shaft. This reduces the final drive speed to 73.63 RPM. This gives a final blade speed of 159 ft. per minute which is a good speed for cutting mild steel. If you cut other materials such as aluminum you can increase the speed of the blade by changing pulleys. We will discuss this in greater detail later in the book.

The pulley drive worked much better than we had anticipated. The reason for this is the adjustable feed pressure control spring. The spring is a 150 pound garage door spring adapted for our purpose. It can be adjusted to control the rate of descent of the vertical frame.

**Figure 5**   Beginning a horizontal cut

Both the drive shaft and the counter shaft are each supported by two 5/8" pillow block bearings.

The 3/4"idler wheel shaft is supported by two 3/4" general purpose ball bearings. The bearings are mounted in a frame and can be adjusted up or down. Using this up and down adjustment we are able to adjust the blade tightness.

The idler wheel also has a tracking adjustment. If the tracking is out of adjustment the blade will not stay on the wheel. The adjustment tilts the idler wheel backward or forward. Adjustments are made until the blade tracks properly on the wheel.

Cutting is accomplished by the continuous blade traveling

around the drive wheel and the idler wheel. The drive and idler wheels are each made from a piece of 3/8" wall 8" diam. pipe. The outside diameter of an 8" pipe measures approximately 8.625 so we were barely able to get the pipe on our 9" lathe. After they are turned on the lathe their final working diameter will be approximately 8-1/4"

The center hubs of both wheels are made of a 1-3/4" length of 1-3/4" diameter round stock. The hub for the drive wheel is bored 5/8". The hub for the idler wheel is bored 3/4". Each wheel is held on the shaft with two 1/4-20 set screws located in each hub.

Both wheels are constructed using a jig to hold the wheel and the hub in their proper position while four 1/2" diam. spokes are welded in place to connect the hub to the wheel. The wheels are then finished on the lathe.

The cutting area of the blade is held in its proper position and supported at the front of the vertical frame by an upper and lower guide roller assembly. The lower guide is stationary, and the upper one is adjustable up or down to accommodate cutting various width material.

Each guide assembly consists of three metal rollers. A roller is located at each side of the blade and at the back of the blade. The blade guide rollers are adjustable. Adjusting the rollers changes the vertical position of the saw blade.

Usually special ball bearings are used as blade guides. But they are expensive so we're going to save a little money and make our own using bronze bushings.

When the saw is used in the vertical position the work is fed through the blade by hand.

During the horizontal cutting process, the work piece is held in the vise. The vertical frame is tilted forward and the moving saw blade comes in contact with the work piece. The weight of the frame provides the feed pressure for the cutting operation.

As mentioned earlier, the feed pressure is controlled by an adjustable spring mounted on the left side of the saw. See fig. 4. One end of the spring is connected to a turn buckle. When the turn buckle is tightened the downward cutting pressure is decreased. When it is loosened, downward cutting pressure is increased.

The carbon flex back blade used on our saw is a 14 teeth per inch raker and is 94" long. Raker means that the teeth are set at a uniform angle, left, right and straight, in sets of three.

## CONSTRUCTION METHODS

As with any project of this type, work is involved, and a lot of it. Before beginning it may help to consider a secret I learned from my Dad a few years ago. Many of you may already know this secret, but I'm a slow learner and it took me 40 years to catch on. The secret is, that any project seems impossible if you look at the whole picture. But if you make a commitment, pick a starting point, develop a positive attitude, and break the job up into small portions it will eventually get done. This idea seems simple and not worth mentioning, but it really works. I know because I'm living proof. You really can know what others know, and do what others do simply by applying yourself. Exciting stuff and I can honestly say that this positive way of thinking changed my life.

**SAWING:** When we started this project we owned one of those cheap import band saws, and we used it to cut the material needed to build our saw. If you are not so lucky and are faced with doing the cutting with a hand hacksaw, don't be discouraged. I have spent my fair share of time using a hand hacksaw and it really is not as bad as it seems, particularly if you develop the attitude I mentioned above.

To make the job as easy as possible you will need either an 18 or 24 TPI high quality flex back blade for the cutting work in this project. I underline high quality because there are cheap, bargain blades available, but they won't do the job. Mount the blade properly in a good quality ridged frame. You will also need a sturdy bench vise for sawing and for a lot of the other handwork that you will be doing in this project

When cutting, take full length strokes at the rate of 60 per minute or less. The actual cutting takes place on the forward stroke, so lift the blade slightly on the back stroke for longer blade life. It takes patience and practice to gain the proper technique. Once the skill is acquired you will find that you are able to cut through a large piece of material in a very short period of time. You may even get so good at sawing by hand you will decide you don't need a power bandsaw after all.

**DRILLING :** An electric hand drill, and a drill press are used for the drilling operations. A complete set of drills 1/8-1/2 will be needed as well as one each of the following sizes: 5/8, 3/4 and 7/8. For the smaller drill sizes it is best to use U.S. made high speed steel drills.

This also holds true with the larger size drills, but they are expensive. If you are not going to use larger sizes on a regular basis you might consider the less expensive import sets available. I bought an inexpensive set of Silver & Demming drills 17/32 - 1" a couple of years ago that were made in China and they have done okay. Not great, just okay.

Most of the assembly holes are 1/4" and can be drilled with the hand drill. But a few are larger, such as the 7/8" hole in each pivot arm and the 3/4" hole for the vise screw shaft. The larger holes are best drilled on a drill press.

Step drilling means to begin a large hole with a small pilot hole and use progressively larger drills to increase the hole to the desired size. This procedure makes the job easier and holds the hole closer to its intended center. It also adds to the life of the larger drills. To step drill a 1/2" hole, punch its center with a center punch. Drill an 1/8" pilot hole, then drill 13/64, 1/4, 5/16, 3/8, 7/16, 15/32, and finally 1/2.

**SAFETY** is important when drilling. There is a danger of loose hair or clothing getting caught in the revolving drill. To prevent this, tie long hair up and don't wear loose clothing. Make sure that the work piece is mounted to the drill table securely in a vise. This prevents the drill from flinging the work piece around when it grabs. Drilling can also cause loose chips of metal to fly through the air, so safety glasses are an absolute necessity. There are many other hidden dangers involved in the drilling process as well as in many other areas of this project. No effort has been made to point them all out, so please proceed with caution and use good common sense in all your shop activities.

**TAPPING:** All of our thread work will be done by hand. The taps required are 1/40-20, 3/8-16, 5/8-11, 7/16-14 and 1/2-13. The only die required is a 1/4-20.

Tapping is a simple process, but it does require patience and plenty of cutting oil. The biggest problem faced is broken taps. The chances of taps breaking can be greatly reduced if you use good quality taps, and if you understand the two main reasons for tap breakage. Those reasons are, starting the tap at an angle and binding caused by chips.

When possible, mount the tap in the drill press chuck and get it started straight by advancing the chuck by hand. When started, carefully remove the tap, and the work from the chuck and finish threading by hand. Advance the tap in quarter turns and back it up from time to time to clear the chips. If it binds work it back and forth until free.

**CUTTING WITH AN OXY-ACETYLENE TORCH...**
Certainly the blade wheel blanks could be cut accurately on a metal lathe using a cut off tool. But the lathe would need to be of sufficient capacity to handle the job, and it would have to be set up to supply a constant flow of coolant to the cutting area.

Since the blade wheel blanks are cut from 3/8" wall, 8" diam. pipe and our lathe was not set up for such a large cut off operation, we used an oxy-acetylene torch. We will outline the general procedure as well as give you a few hints on this subject. But you must realize, it would be possible to write several books on the safety and proper use of a cutting torch and still not completely cover the issue. For that reason, we must assume that you are experienced in its use and if not, suggest that you either check with your local library and review one of the many books available on the subject and/or enroll in a welding class.

**SAFETY** is the most important thing to keep in mind when using an Oxy-Acetylene Torch. Before starting to cut, make sure that there are no materials nearby, or openings leading to material, that flame, sparks, hot metal or slag might ignite. Always wear protective goggles supplied by a reputable manufacture. Keep a clear space between the cylinders and the work. To prevent burns do not use matches when lighting blow pipes. Use friction lighters. Many types of clothing are extremely flammable, so pay particular attention to what you are wearing. Clothing should be fireproof or at the very least resistant to sparks and hot slag. Be sure that proper and adequate ventilation is supplied to your work area by natural means or by an air fan or blower. These and many other precautions are necessary when working with a torch. Another good idea is to keep a bucket of sand and water close by in case something goes wrong. And no shop should be without a fully serviced fire extinguisher. Once again, there are hidden dangers in any shop activity. I am unable to point out all of them to you, so please use extreme caution and common sense.

**LATHE WORK:** All of the lathe work done in this project is of a simple nature and is done on a 9" lathe. A few boring, facing and turning operations are all that are required.

The lathe is used to face off the blade wheels and hubs. The outside surface of the blade wheel is also turned to its proper shape and size on the lathe. Boring operations include the blade wheel hubs, the six blade guide rollers and the eccentric guide roller adjustment bolts.

A detailed description of lathe operation is beyond the scope of this book, so we must assume that you know how to run a lathe and are familiar with safety rules involved with its operation. If you are not, we suggest that you study one of the many good manuals on lathe operation. One such book is South Bend's, "How To Run A Lathe", Available from Lindsay Publications, P.O. Box 538, Bradley, IL 60915-0538.

You will need a 6", 3 jaw universal geared chuck and a 6", 4 jaw independent chuck. I won't make any special mention of the work turned in the 3 jaw chuck because it is automatically centered.

Centering in the 4 jaw chuck is a different story. The work is first centered approximately, using the concentric rings scribed in the face of the chuck as markers. The lathe is started and the work is marked, either by a piece of chalk, or by slowly advancing the cutting tool until it just touches the revolving work. The lathe is stopped and the jaw opposite the mark made by the chalk or cutting tool is loosened slightly, and the jaw opposite of it is tightened. This procedure is continued until the work is centered. A dial test indicator can also be used for centering a piece of work.

For drilling operations on the lathe a 1/2" drill chuck is mounted on the tail stock.

The blade wheel hubs are bored using a 1/2" boring bar. You can order boring tools from most tool supply catalogs or you can save some money by making your own from drill rod. Drill rod is available in 36" lengths from most industrial supply houses.

A boring bar can be made by heating the end of 6" length of drill rod to a bright red and forging a small hook on the end. The end is hardened and tempered by quenching it quickly in oil or water. Ask what quenching method to use when you buy your rod.

The tool is ground on the hook end exactly the same as the left hand turning tool, except the front clearance must be ground at a slightly greater angle so that the heel of the tool will not rub in the hole of the work.

The tool end will be brittle if left fully hardened, so it must be tempered. Reheat the end to a straw color, then quench it. The cutting edge can be improved by honing.

**WELDING:** There are a few items that require welding such as the spokes in the blade wheels, The table ends and a couple of other areas that I'll mention later on. These welds will be single pass filet welds. A welder capable of at least 75 amps will be required.

**OTHER TOOLS REQUIRED:** Several common hand tools are necessary to assemble the saw. A set of combination wrenches 3/8 through 3/4. An 8" adjustable wrench. A couple of pairs of vise grips, several 4" "C" clamps, an assortment of screw drivers, set of Allen wrenches 1/8 - 3/8", a "T" square, straight edge, level and a tape measure. You'll also need a center punch, scratch awl and a hammer. A 0-180 degree round head protractor with an 8" arm was used to measure the angle bends necessary in this project.

## MATERIAL LIST:

2 - pieces of 5/16 x 3 flat bar 8-1/2" long. (*Saw table end pieces*).

2 - pieces of 1/4 x 3 x 4 angle 36" long. (*Table top*).

2 - pieces of 1/8 x 1-1/2 angle 24" long. (*Front legs*).

2 - pieces of 1/8 x 1-1/2 angle 22" long. (*Middle legs*).

2 - pieces of 1/8 x 1-1/2 angle 25" long. (*Rear legs*).

1 - piece of 1/8 x 1-1/2 angle 8-1/2" long. (*Front leg bottom brace*).

2 - pieces of 1/8 x 1-1/2 angle 14" long. (*Lower middle-rear leg brace*).

1 - piece of 1/8 x 1-1/2 angle 8-1/2" long. (*Front leg base*).

1 - piece of 1/4 x 2 angle 22" long. (*Rear leg base*).

6 - pieces of 1/8 x 3/4 strap iron 12" long. (*Leg cross braces*).

2 - pieces of 1/8 x 3/4 strap iron 5" long. (*Upper middle leg brace*).

## MATERIAL LIST CONTINUED:

2 - pieces of 1/8 x 1-1/2 angle 12" long. *(Landing gear legs).*

1 - piece of 1/8 x 1-1/2 angle 21" long. *(Landing gear cross brace).*

1 - piece of 1/2 round rod 26" long. *(Landing gear wheel axle).*

2 - pieces of 1/8 x 3/4 strap iron 3" long. *(Landing gear hinge post).*

1 - piece of 1/2 round rod 10-1/2" long. *(Landing gear hinge bar).*

2 - 6" metal hub lawn mower wheels with 3/4" wide tread and a 1/2" axle bore. *(Wheels for landing gear).*

2 - pieces of 1/8 x 1 strap iron 12" long. *(Lock bar side arms).*

1 - piece of 1/4 dia. round rod 10-1/4" long. *(Lock bar handle).*

1 - piece of 5/8-11 threaded rod 14" long. *(Vise travel bolt).*

2 - pieces of 1/4 x 1-1/2 x 2 angle 3-1/2" long. *(Travel nuts).*

1 - piece of 1/4 x 2 flat bar 4" long. *(Vise guide plate).*

1 - piece of 3/8 x 3 flat bar 6" long. *(Vise top spacer plate).*

1 - piece of 3/8 x 1-1/2 flat bar 17" long. *(Clamp bar).*

## MATERIAL LIST CONTINUED:

1 - piece of 3/8 x 3 angle 7-1/2" long. *(Vise clamp).*

1 - piece of 1/4 x 3 flat bar 3-1/2" long. *(Clamp guide plate).*

1 - piece of 3/8 x 3 angle 9" long. *(Stationary vise clamp).*

1 - piece of 3/8 x 1 flat bar 3-1/2" long. *(Stop plate).*

1 - piece of 7/8 round rod 14-1/4" long. *(Pivot hinge pin).*

1 - piece of 3/8 x 2 flat bar 25" long. *(Left side pivot arm).*

1 - piece of 3" channel 48" long. *(Vertical post).*

1 - piece of 1/4 x 2 angle 35" long. *(Vertical post brace).*

1 - piece of 3/8 x 1-1/2 flat bar 15-3/4" long. *(Right side pivot arm).*

1 - piece of 1/4 x 2 angle 16" long. *(Lower section top brace).*

1 - piece of 1/8 x 1-1/2 angle 16" long. *(Lower section middle brace).*

1 - piece of 1/8 x 1-1/2 angle 22-3/4" long. *(Lower section bottom cross brace).*

1 - piece of 1/8 x 1-1/2 angle 19" long. *(Frame rail).*

3 - pieces of 1/8 x 1-1/2 angle 4-3/8" long. *(Cross braces).*

## MATERIAL LIST CONTINUED:

1 - piece of 1/8 x 1-1/2 angle 8" long. *(Drive assembly corner post)*.

2- pieces of 1/4 x 3/4 flat bar 4-3/4" long. *(Drive assembly cross brace)*.

1 - piece of 3/8 x 3/4 flat bar 8" long. *(Drive assembly corner post)*.

1 - piece of 1/8 x 1-1/2 angle 9" long. *(Outer drive frame rail)*

2 - pieces of 1/8 x 1-1/2 angle 6-1/2" long. *(Motor mount base rails)*

2 - pieces of 1/8 x 1-1/2 angle 10-1/2" long. *(Motor mount side rails)*.

3 - pieces of 1/8 x 1 strap iron 4" long. *(Rail spreader)*.

2 - pieces of 1/8 x 1-1/2 angle 6-1/2" long. *(Motor mount rail)*.

1 - piece 1/4 x 2 flat bar 13-1/2" long. *(Inside brace, upper vertical frame)*.

1 - piece of 1/4 x 1-1/2 flat bar 14" long. *(Right side, upper section, lower frame rail)*.

2 - pieces of 1/8 x 1-1/2 angle 2" long. *(Mounting brackets for inside frame)*.

## MATERIAL LIST CONTINUED:

2 - pieces of 1/4 x 1-1/2 angle 14" long. *(Upper section right and left frame rails).*

1 - piece of 3" channel 13" long. *(Front upper frame post).*

1 - piece of 1/4 x 4 flat bar 5" long. *(Back plate for adjustable track).*

2 - pieces of 1/4 x 3/4 flat bar 13" long. *(track for adjustable blade assembly).*

2 - pieces of 1/8 x 1 angle 14" long. *(Rails for blade roller assembly).*

1 - piece of 1/8 x 1 angle 2-1/2" long. *(Bottom rail spreader).*

1 - piece of 1/8 x 1 strap iron 2-1/2" long. *(Top rail spreader).*

1 - piece of 3/8 x 1-1/2 flat bar 7" long. *(Upper blade wheel adjustment arm).*

2 - pieces of 1/2 x 1/2 bar stock 13" long. *(Inside rails for upper blade wheel bearing assembly).*

2 - pieces of 1/2 x 1/2 bar stock 2-3/4" long. *(Cross braces).*

2 - pieces of 1/2 x 1/2 bar stock 6-3/4" long. *(Outside frame rails).*

## MATERIAL LIST CONTINUED:

1 - piece of 1-1/4 black pipe 3-1/2" long, threaded on one side. *(Idler wheel bearing housing)*.

1 - piece of 7/8 diam. round rod 10" long. *(Idler wheel shaft)*.

1 - piece of 1-1/2 black pipe 3-1/2" long. *(Yoke)*.

1 - piece of 5/8 diam. round rod 7" long. *(Drive shaft)*.

1 - piece of 5/8 diam. round rod 10" long. *(Countershaft)*.

1 - piece of 1/4 x 1-1/2 flat bar 4-1/2" long. *(Pillow block spacer)*.

1 - piece of 1-1/2 round rod 6" long. *(Guide blade rollers)*.

1 - piece of 3" channel 3-1/2" long. *(Lower blade guide mounting base)*.

1 - piece of 1/4 x 1-1/2 angle 1-1/2" long. *(Rear roller mounting bracket)*.

1 - piece of 1/4 x 2 flat bar 4-3/4" long. *(Mounting bracket for lower blade guide roller base)*.

1 - piece of 5-1/2 x 3-1/2, 12 GA hot roll sheet steel. *(Work table)*.

1 - piece of 1/4 x 4 flat bar 4-1/2" long. *(Mounting plate for upper blade guide roller assembly)*.

## MATERIAL LIST CONTINUED:

1 - piece of 1-1/2 x 2 angle 3-1/2" long. *(Upper blade guide base).*

1 - piece of 1/4 x 1-1/2 angle 1" long. *(Rear guide roller bracket).*

2 - pieces of 8" I.D. pipe 1-1/4" long. *(Blade wheels).*

8 - pieces of 1/2" round rod 3-1/8" long. *(Spokes for blade wheels).*

2 - pieces of 1-3/4" diam. round rod 1-3/4" long. *(Blade wheel hubs).*

1 - piece of 3/4" x 12 x 12 plywood. *(Blade wheel jig).*

4 - pieces of 1/8 x 1" angle 1-1/2" long. *(Blade wheel jig).*

8 - pieces of 1/8 x 3/4 angle 1-1/2" long. *(Blade wheel jig).*

4 - pieces of 1/8 x 1/2 strap 1-1/2" long. *(Blade wheel jig).*

Approximately 100, 1/4-20 x 1 bolts with nuts and lock washers.

Approximately 25, 1/4-20 x 1-1/2 bolts with nuts and lock washers.

Four 1/2" flat washers.

## MATERIAL LIST CONTINUED:

Four 1/8 x 1 cotter pins.

One - 5/8-11 x 2 coupling nut.

Two - 5/8 flat washers.

Six - 5/8 set screw collars.

Two - 5/8-11 nuts.

Two - 1/2-13 x 2 socket head bolts.

One - 1/2-13 x 8 bolt with nuts.

Five - 3/8-16 X 2 bolts with nuts and lock washers.

Five - 7/8 set screw collars.

Two - 3/8-16 x 1 bolts with nuts and lock washers.

Two - 3/8 I.D. bushings 7/8" long.

Two - 3/8 flat washers.

Two - 3/4 bore general purpose bearings.

One - 1/2" set screw collar.

One, 1/2-13 x 1-3/4 coupling nut.

Two- 5/8 bore solid mount bronze sleeved pillow block bearings

## MATERIAL LIST CONTINUED:

One - 5/8 bore 6" A-size pulley.

Two - 5/8 bore resilient mount pillow block bearings.

One - 5/8 bore 8" A-size pulley.

One - 5/8 bar 1-3/4 A-size pulley.

One - 1/2 H.P. 1750 RPM 120 volt electric motor. *(Must be able to run in a counter clockwise direction).*

Two - 30" "V" belts.

One - 1/2 bore 1-1/2 A-size pulley.

Six - 1/2-13 x 3 grade 6 bolts.

Six - 5/8 I.D. bronze bushings 7/16" long.

Six - 3/8-16 x 1 cap screws.

Two - 1/4-20 x 1/2 socket head counter sink bolts.

One - 3/8-16 x 1-1/2 bolt with nut and lock washer.

One - 10" turn buckle.

One - 150 lb. garage door spring having at least 9" of coil length.

One - 7/8 X 2-3/4 "S" hook.

## MATERIAL LIST CONTINUED:

One - 1" eye bolt with a 3/8-16 shank, with two 3/8 nuts.

Four - 1/4-20 x 1 set screws.

Four - #6 counter sink wood screws 1/2" long.

Four - 1/4 lag bolts 1-1/2" long.

Four - 1/4 lag bolts 2" long.

**DRAWING NOTES:** Some of you may not be used to reading drawing dimensions using decimals instead of fractions. For that reason I have included the conversion table located below.

Another thing that may not be familiar, is the circle with a line through it ( ⌀ ) located in many of the drawings. This symbol means the same as diameter. ⌀.75 is the same as .75 diameter. Refering to more than one hole in a drawing with the same diameter would look like this, (⌀.75 x 2).

### DECIMAL CONVERSION TABLE

| | |
|---|---|
| 1/16 = .0625 | 1/2 = .5 |
| 1/8 = .125 | 9/16 = .5625 |
| 3/16 = .1875 | 5/8 = .625 |
| 1/4 = .25 | 11/16 = .6875 |
| 5/16 = .3125 | 3/4 = .75 |
| 3/8 = .375 | 13/16 = .8125 |
| 7/16 = .4375 | 7/8 = .875 |

# SECTION 1

## BUILDING THE BASE

**THE TABLE TOP:** We will begin our project by constructing the table top. Cut 2 pieces of 5/16 x 3 flat bar 8-1/2" long as shown in fig. 6. These are the table end plates. Drill a 3/4" hole in one of the plates in the location shown. The plate with the hole will be the front plate. The hole is for the threaded rod that controls the vise. The other plate is the rear plate and it is left blank.

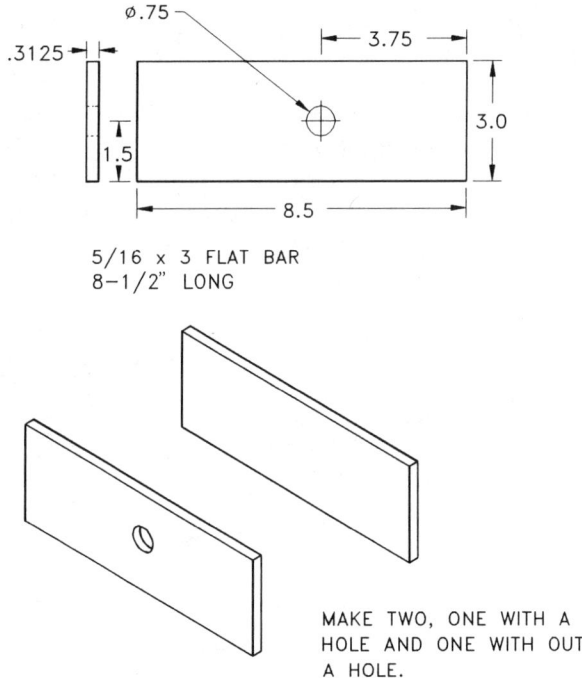

**Figure 6** End plates. The plate with the hole is located at the front of the table. The blank plate is located at the rear of the table

Make the saw table from two pieces of 1/4 x 3 x 4 angle 36" long. The right side table top is shown in fig.7. Notice that the 3" wide section forms the top, and the 4" wide section forms the side.

Drill the following holes in the locations shown in fig.7. A 3/8" hole in the top for the vise jaw. The six 1/4" holes in the side for the legs. The 7/8" hole is for the vertical frame pivot rod. It's best to use a drill press to step drill the larger holes.

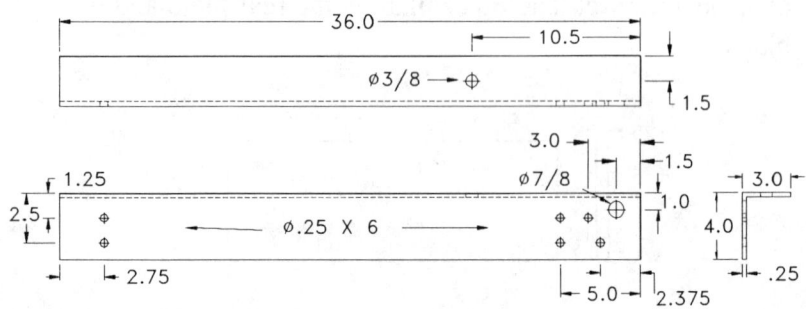

1/4 X 3 X 4 ANGLE 36" LONG

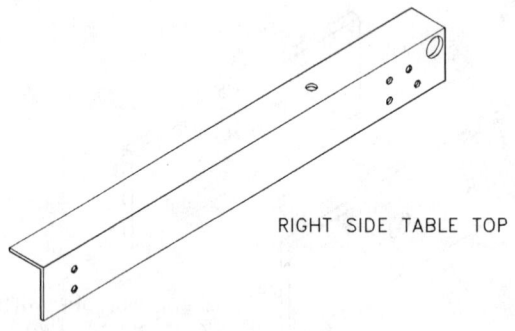

RIGHT SIDE TABLE TOP

**Figure 7**     **Right side table top**

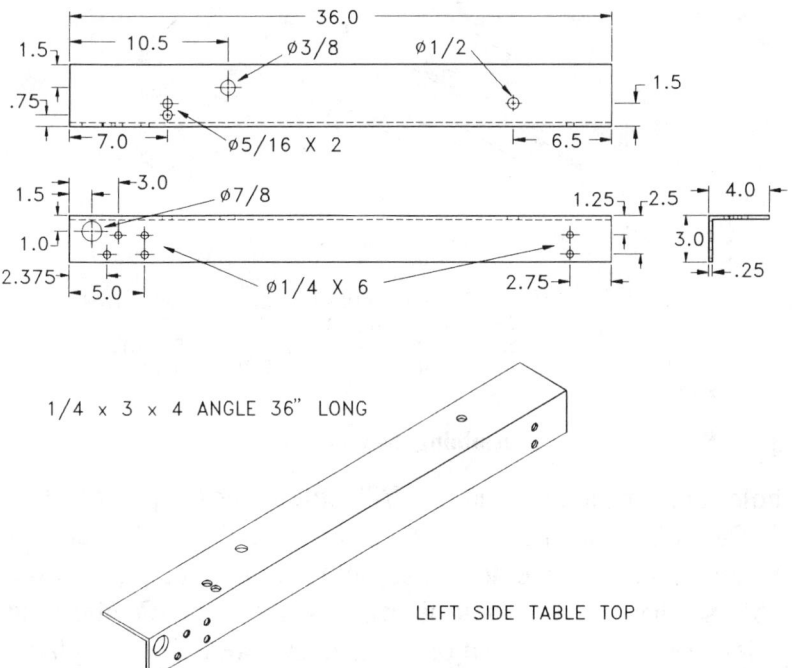

**Figure 8**  Left side table top

Fig. 8 shows the left side table top. Notice that on this side the 4" wide section forms the table top, and the 3" wide section forms the side.

The following holes are drilled in the top as shown. A 1/2" hole for the stop bolt. A 3/8" hole for the vise, and the two 5/16" holes are for the vertical stop bracket. The six 1/4" side

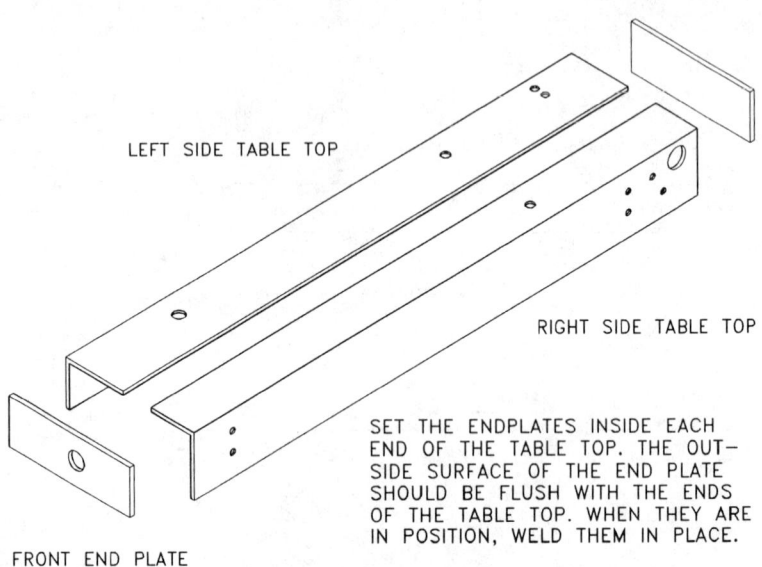

**Figure 9**     Assembling the table top

holes are for the legs and the 7/8" hole is for the pivot rod.

The table top is put together as shown in fig. 9. Notice that the end plate with the hole is set in position at the front of the table so that the 3/4" hole is offset to the right. Position the plates flush inside each end of the table and weld them in place.

**THE TABLE LEGS:** There are three sets of legs that hold the table up. They are, the front legs, the middle legs and the rear legs. Make each set of legs as an opposing pair.

The front legs are 24" long and are shown in fig. 10. Drill two 1/4" holes in the top of each leg. The legs are bolted to the table using these holes. Drill the 1/4" hole at the bottom of each leg. These are for mounting the front leg base.

The middle legs are 22" long and are shown in fig. 11. Drill two 1/4" mounting holes in the top of each leg. These holes are

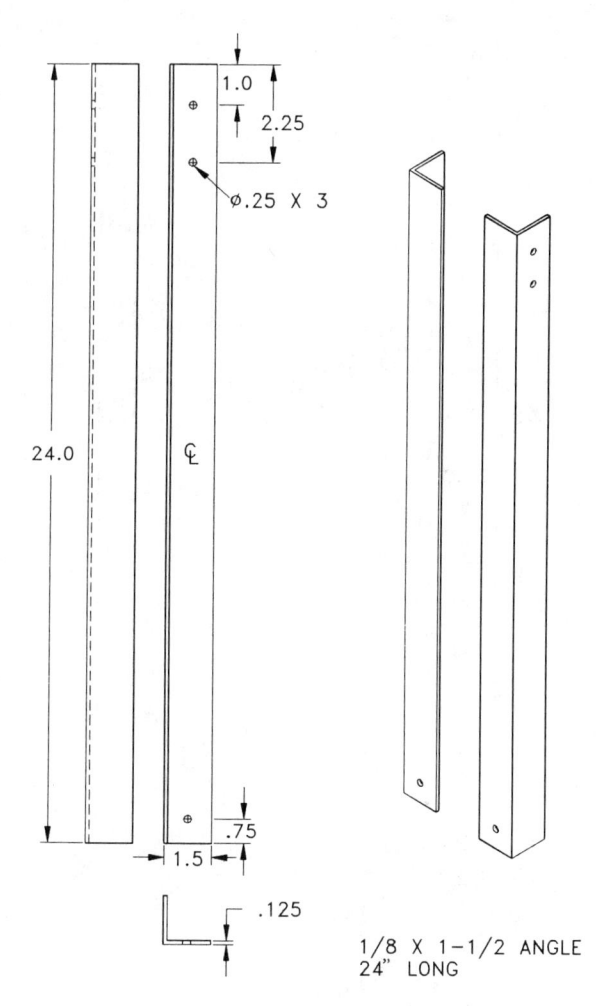

**Figure 10**     **Front legs. Make an opposing pair**

for mounting the legs to the table top.

The rear legs are shown in fig. 12. Notice that both ends of each of these legs are cut off at a 65 degree angle. The angle cut can be marked with a protractor.

It's much easier to mark and drill the holes before you cut

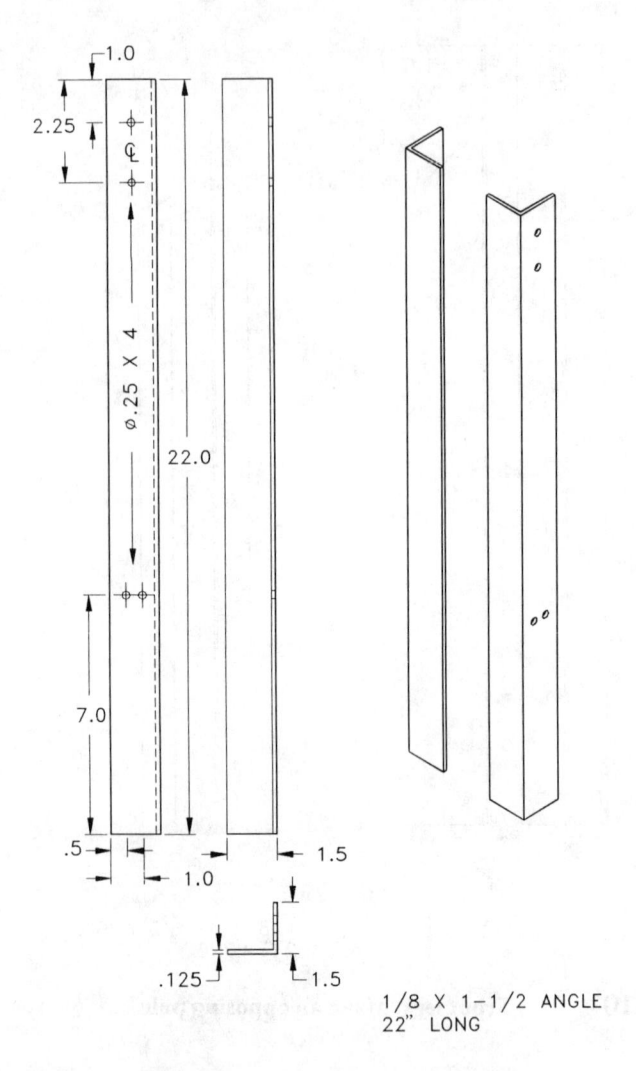

**Figure 11**     Middle legs. Make and opposing pair

the angles. Drill the two 1/4" holes in the top of the leg in the location shown. The legs are mounted to the table using these holes. Drill the 1/4" hole in the bottom of each leg for the leg brace.

38

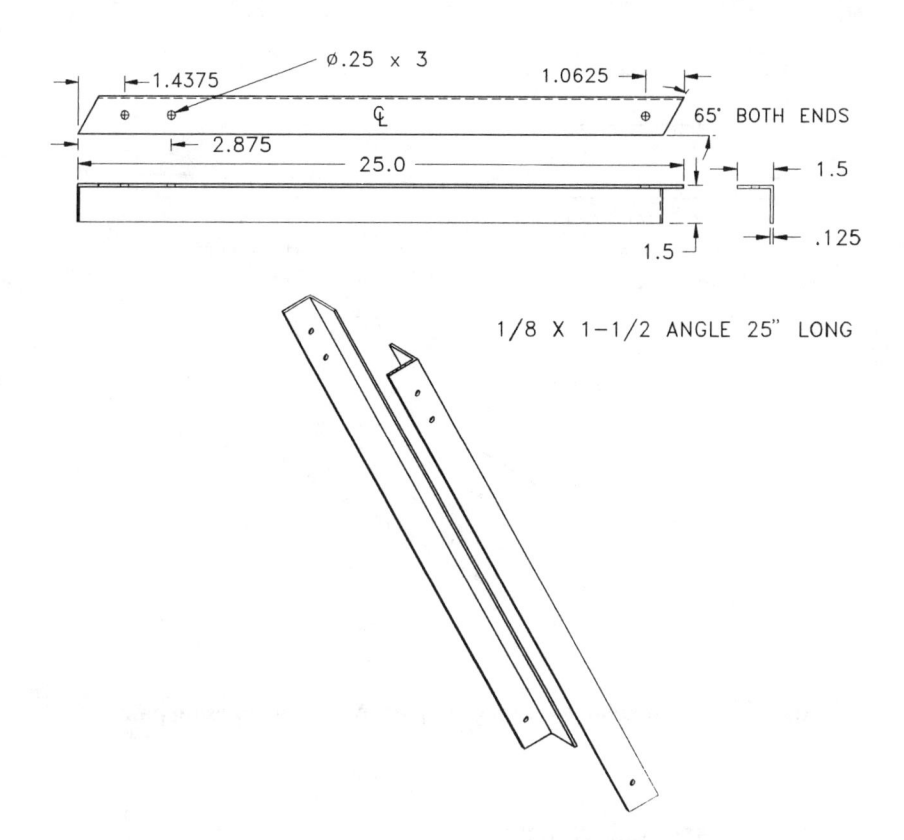

**Figure 12**     Rear legs. Make an opposing pair

Fig. 13 shows the braces that give support to the middle and rear legs. Make them from 1/8 x 1-1/2 angle 14" long. Drill three 1/4" mounting holes in each one.

Fig. 14 shows the front leg base. It is made from a piece of 1/8 x 1-1/2 angle 8-1/2 " long. Drill two 1/4" holes in the base as shown.

Bolt the front, middle and rear legs to the saw table as shown in fig. 16. Use 1/4-20 x 1 bolts, nuts and lockwashers.

Bolt the front leg brace to the front legs with 1/4-20 x 1

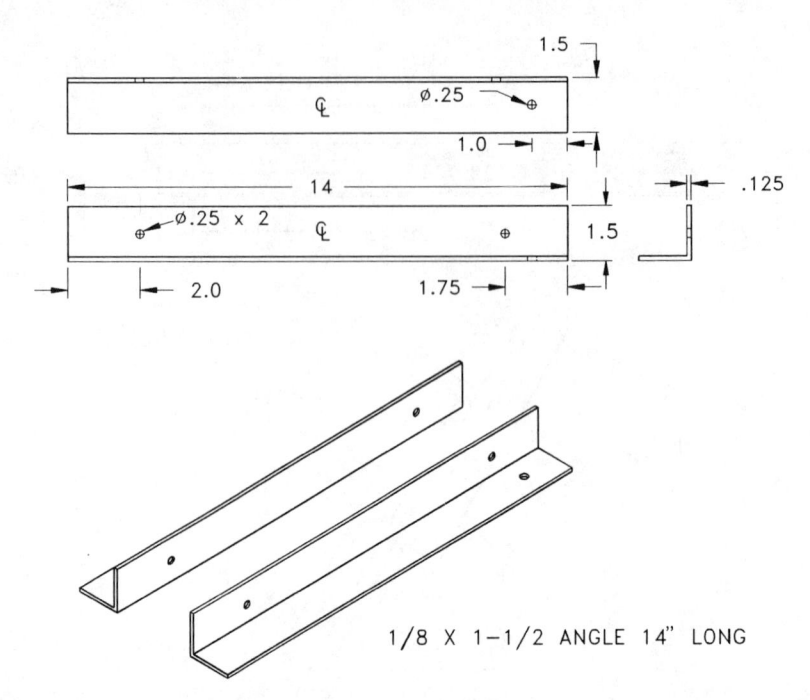

**Figure 13**  Middle to rear leg support. Make an opposing pair

bolts, nuts and lockwashers.

Bolt one end of the middle to rear leg support to the rear legs with 1/4-20 x 1 bolts, nuts and lockwashers. Align the edges of the other end of the middle to rear leg support with the bottom of the middle leg and weld them together as shown in fig 16. The reason we weld the brace to the middle leg is to allow clearance for the landing gear lock bar. A bolt head sticking out would prevent the lock bar from dropping to the lock position.

Cut 6 pieces of 1/8 x 3/4 strap iron 12" long as shown in fig. 15. These are the cross braces and they strengthen the front, middle and rear legs.

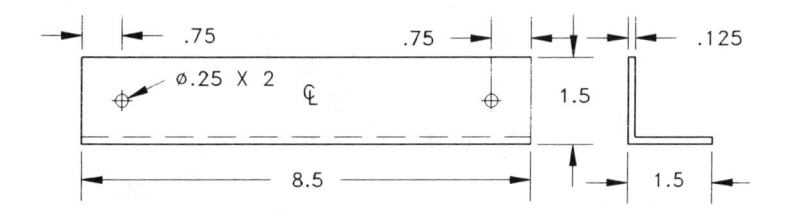

1-1/2 X 1/8 ANGLE 8-1/2" LONG

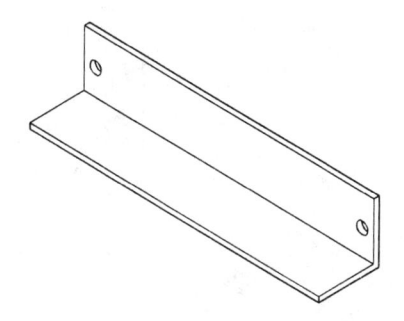

**Figure 14**    **Front leg brace**

1/8 X 3/4 STRAP 12" LONG

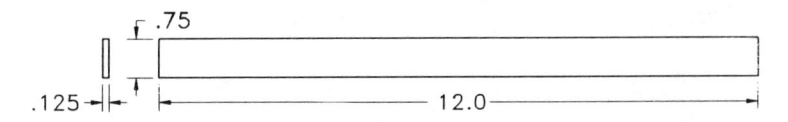

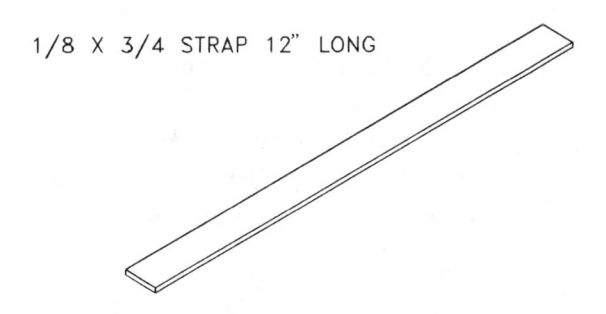

**Figure 15**    **Front, middle and rear leg cross braces. Make six.**

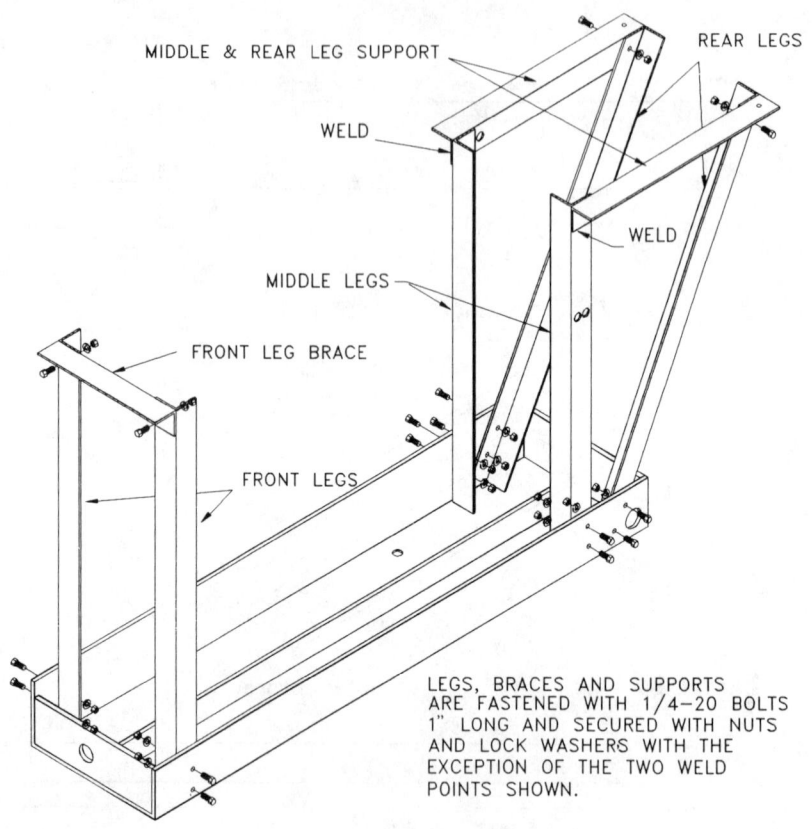

**Figure 16**  Mounting the legs to the saw table

The top middle to rear leg brace is shown in fig. 17. Make 2 braces from 1/8 x 3/4 strap 5" long.

The rear leg base is shown in fig. 18. Make it by cutting a piece of 1/4 x 2 angle 22" long. Drill two 1/4" holes in the locations shown. These holes are used to mount the base to the rear legs.

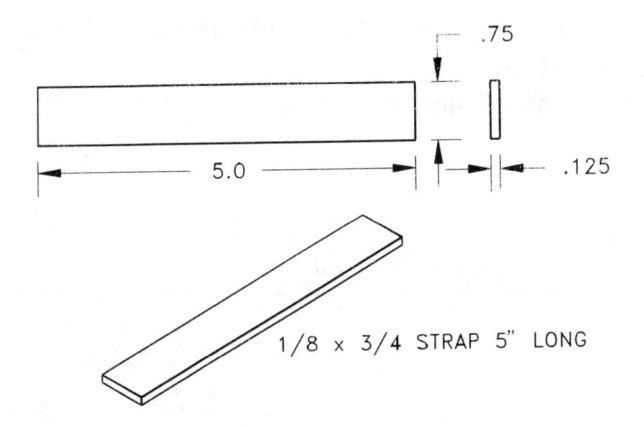

**Figure 17**  Middle to rear leg upper cross brace. Make 2

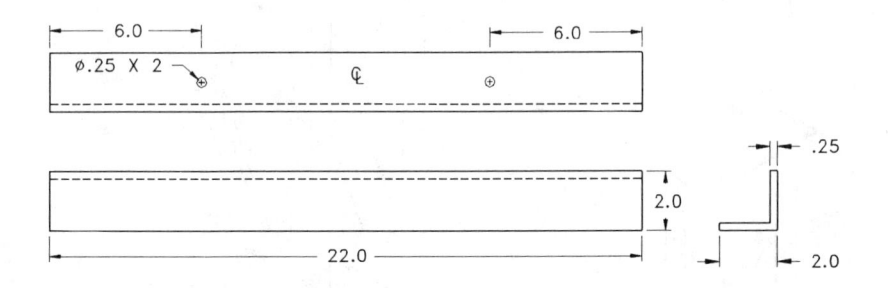

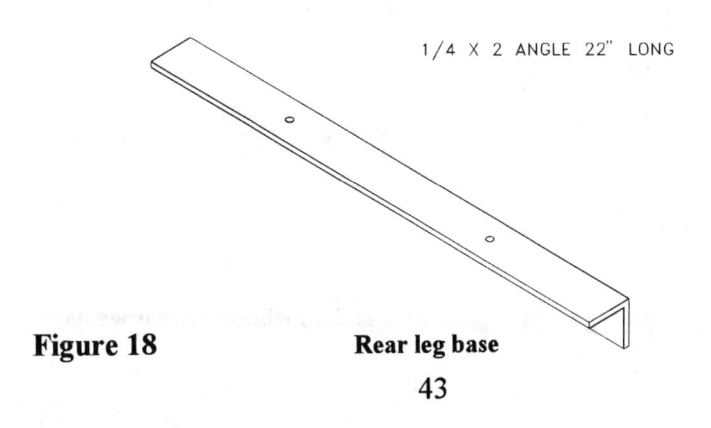

**Figure 18**  Rear leg base

43

Bolt the rear base to the rear leg brace before welding the cross braces to the legs. Mount the base with 1/4-20 x 1 bolts, nuts and lockwashers. See fig. 19.

The locations of the cross braces are not critical. Just

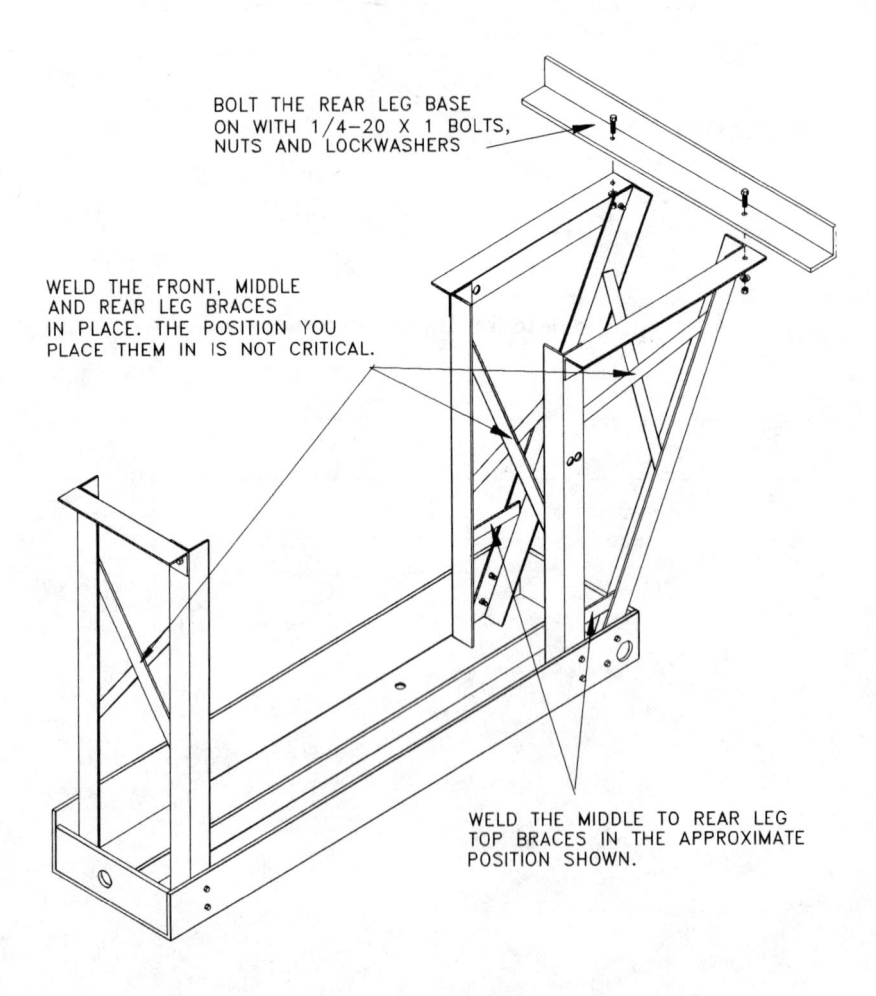

**Figure 19** **Welding in the cross braces and attaching the rear leg base**

position them approximately in the center of each pair of legs so that they form an "X". Clamp them in position with "C" clamps or vise grips and weld.

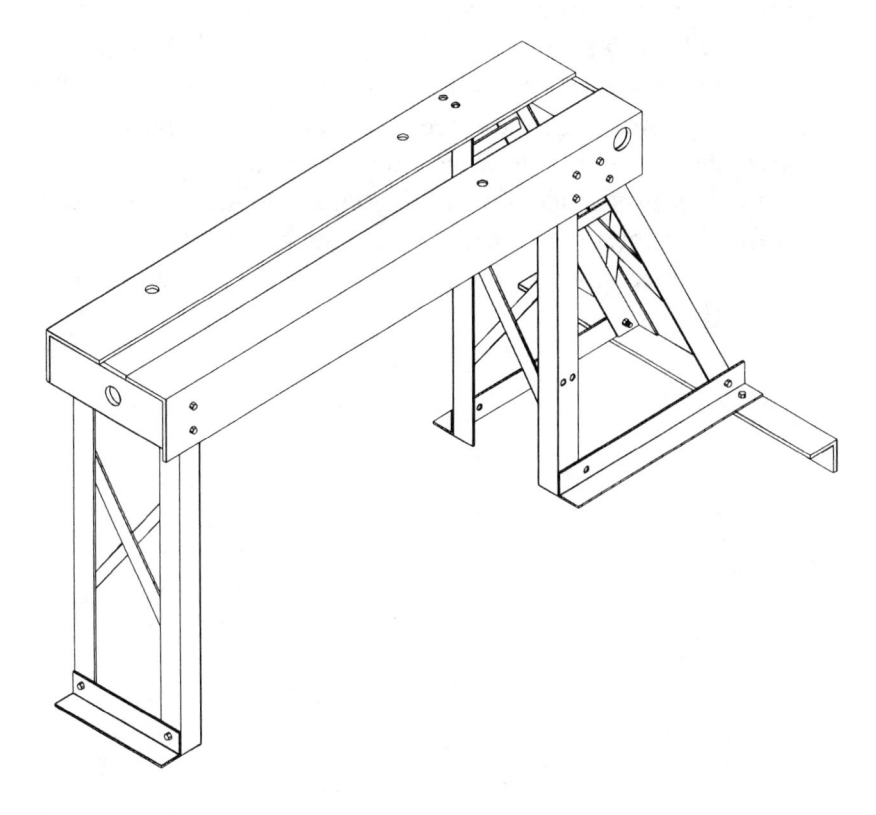

**Figure 20**           Saw table complete

Position the middle to rear top leg braces in the approximate position shown in fig 19. Clamp them in place and weld.

Congratulations, you have successfully completed the saw table. Turn the saw over so that it is right side up. It should look something like the drawing in fig. 20.

**BUILDING THE LANDING GEAR:** From now on I will refer to the wheel assembly as the landing gear. I do this because it kind of reminds me of the wheels on an airplane.

To operate the landing gear, lift the front end of the table up and the wheels will drop down and lock in position. With the wheels in the locked position the saw can be rolled to another location. To disengage the wheels, lift the front of the saw and release the lock bar. The wheels will drop out of position.

Fig. 21 shows a side view of the wheels in the lock position and fig. 22 shows the wheels in the unlocked position.

Cut two pieces of 1/8 x 1-1/2 angle 12" long. These will be

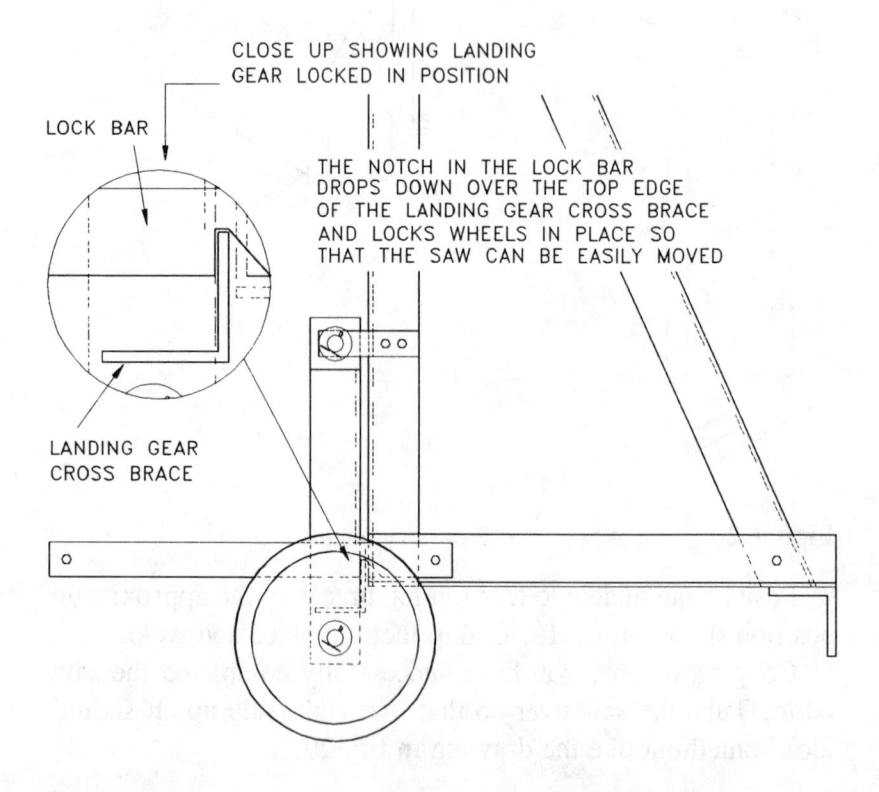

**Figure 21**  Side view of landing gear in locked position

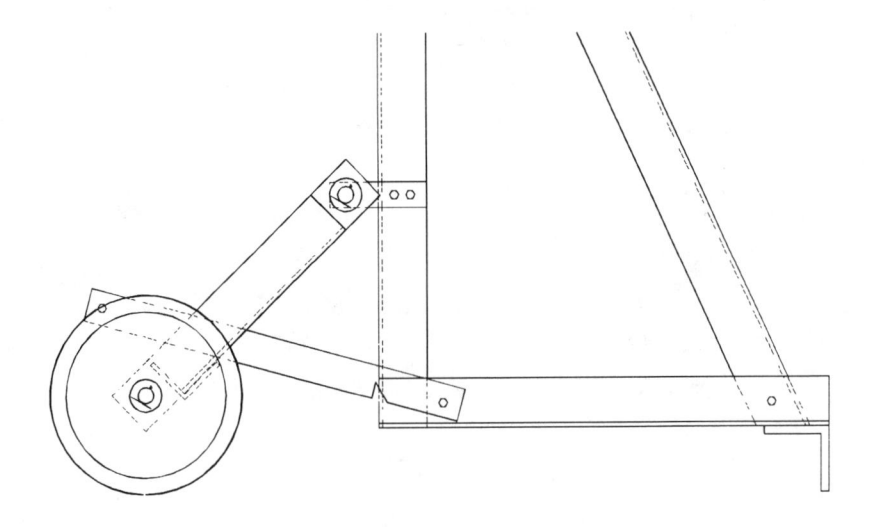

**Figure 22**     Landing gear in unlocked position

the landing gear legs and we will need an opposing pair.

Before making any of the cuts or bends, drill the two 1/2" holes for the axle and the two 1/2" holes for the hinge bar as shown if fig. 23. Then make the cuts in each end as shown.

Make the angle bends by putting one end of the leg in a vise and bending it to a 45 degree angle. The 1/8" material bends very easy so it is not necessary to apply any heat to the bend. Check the angle with a protractor as you make the bend. Put the other end of the same leg in the vise and bent it to the same angle in the opposite direction. See fig.23.

The landing gear hinges are each made from a piece of 1/8 x 3/4 x 3 strap iron. Drill two 1/4" mounting holes in one end of each hinge as shown in fig. 25. Drill a 1/2" hole in the other end of each hinge for the hinge rod.

Cut a piece of 1/8 x 1-1/2 angle 21" long. This is the landing gear cross brace and it is shown in fig. 24.

BEND THE ENDS IN OPPOSITE DIRECTIONS

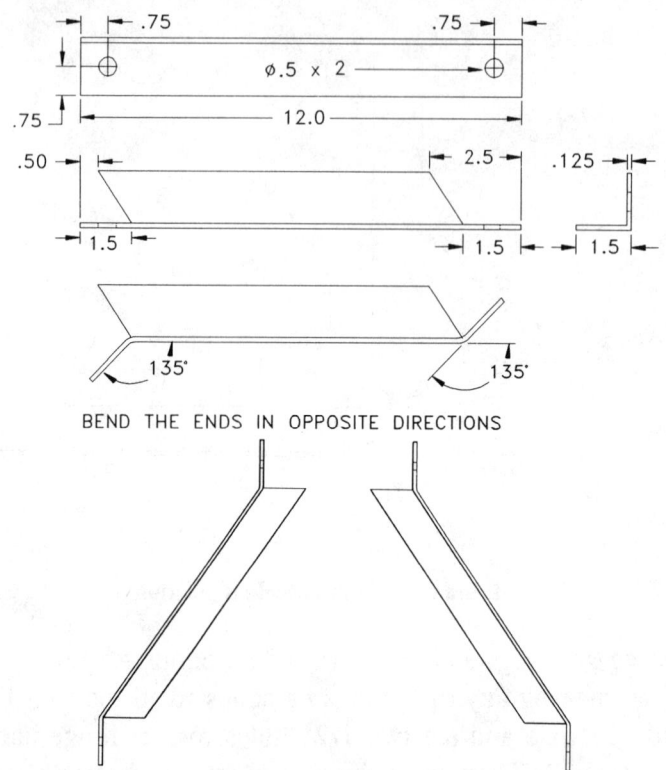

**Figure 23**     Landing gear legs. Make an opposing pair

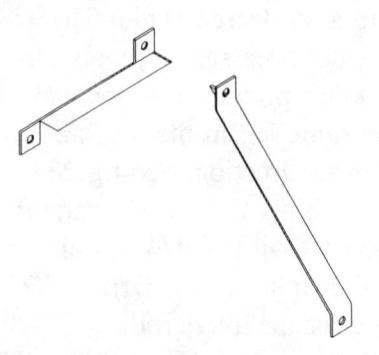

**Figure 23A**     Perspective view of landing gear legs

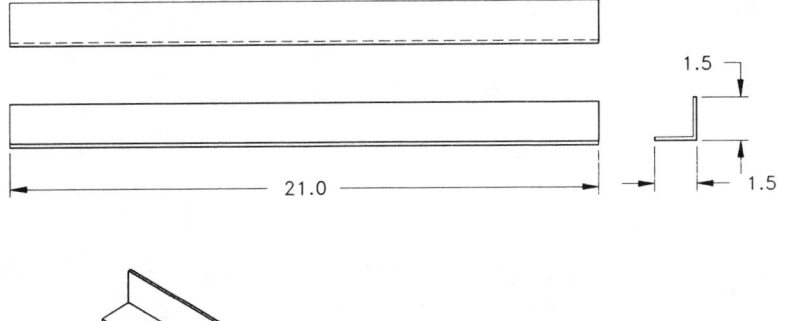

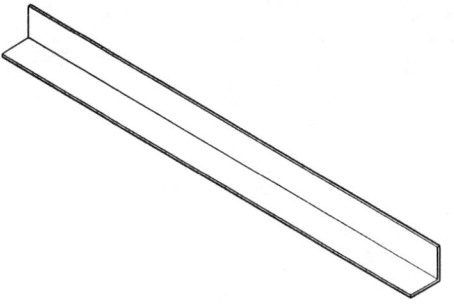

**Figure 24**     Landing gear cross brace

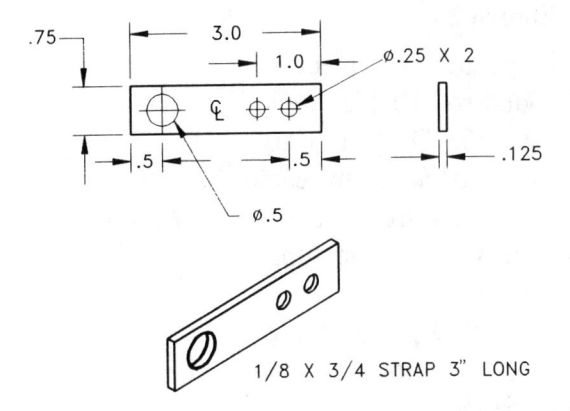

**Figure 25**     Landing gear hinge. Make 2

49

```
⌀.1875 X 2                    ⌀.5
                    .125
         10.5
```

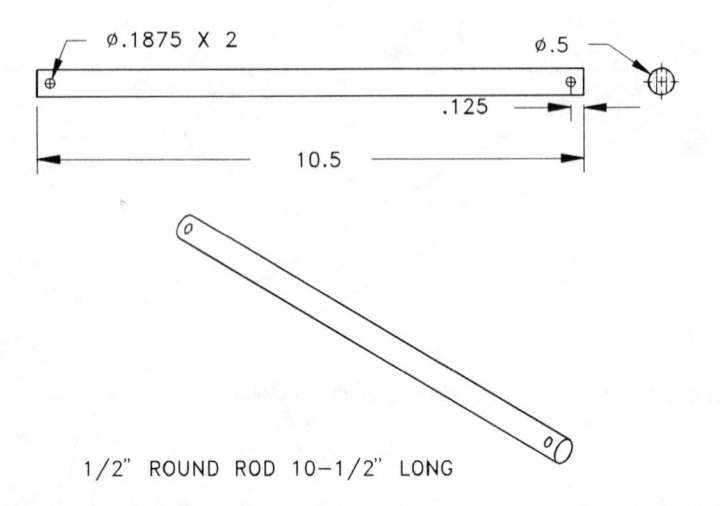

1/2" ROUND ROD 10-1/2" LONG

**Figure 26**     Hinge bar

The hinge bar is a piece of 1/2" round rod 10-1/2" long. See fig. 26. Drill a 3/16" hole 1/8" back from each end. The holes are for cotter pins which hold the hinge bar in place.

Cut another piece of 1/2" round rod 26" long for the wheel axle. See fig. 28. Drill a 3/16" hole 1/8" back from each end for the cotter pins.

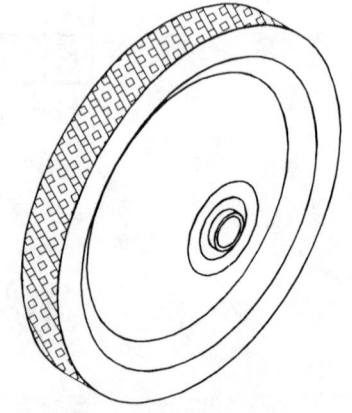

**Figure 27**     6" Wheel

Cut a piece of 1/4" round rod 10-1/4" long for the lock bar

**Figure 28**     **Wheel axle**

1/2" ROUND ROD 26" LONG

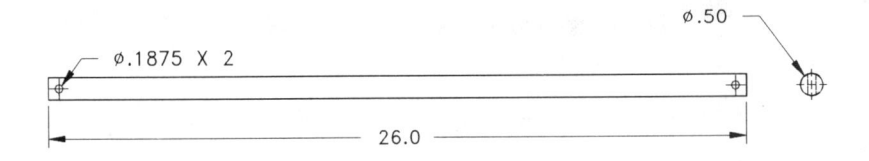

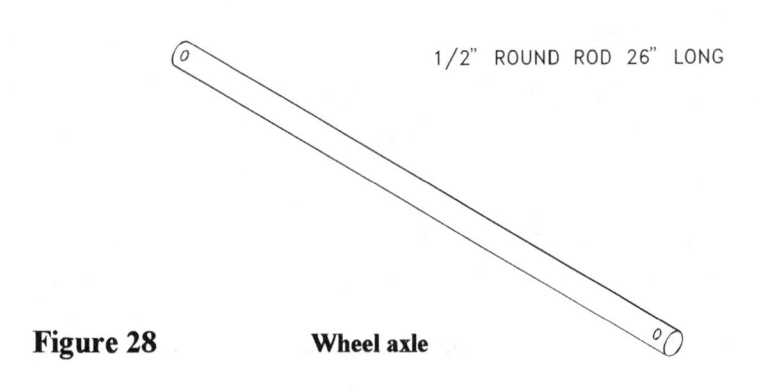

Ø.1875 X 2     26.0     Ø.50

handle. Thread each end 1/4-20 as shown in fig. 29.

The lock bars are shown in fig.30. Make two of them from 1/8 x 1 strap 12" long. Cut a notch in each one as shown. The purpose of the notch is to lock the landing gear in place.

Drill two 1/4"holes in each bar. The 1/4" hole closest to the notch is for mounting the lock bar to the middle leg. The other 1/4" hole is for mounting the lockbar handle.

The two wheels used on the saw are 6", metal hub, lawn mower wheels with a 1/2" axle bore. The tread on these wheels is 3/4" wide. A drawing of the wheel is shown in fig. 27.

You can find these wheels at most hardware stores, But they cost about $5.00 or $6.00 a each. If you can borrow a couple from an old discarded lawnmower you'll save a few bucks.

THREADED BOTH ENDS 1/4–20

⌀.25

|← 1.0 →|     |← 1.0 →|

|←————— 10.25 —————→|

1/4" ROUND ROD 10-1/4" LONG
THREADED 1/4–20 ON BOTH ENDS

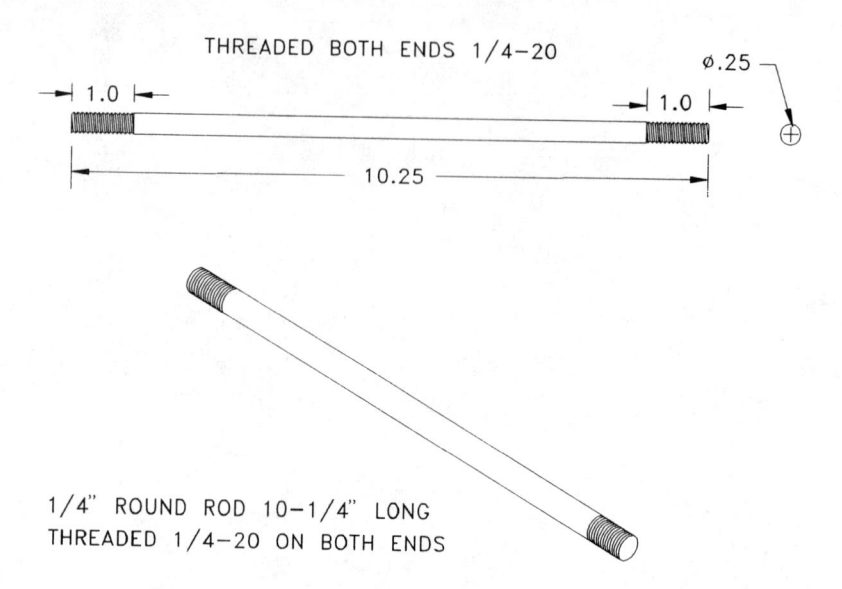

**Figure 29**     **Lock bar handle**

|←———— 12.0 ————→|  .50  |→|   1.0

⌀.25 X 2    ℄

.50    |←2.25→|
       |←2.75→|   .125

THE PURPOSE OF THIS
NOTCH CUT OUT IS TO
ENABLE THE WHEEL
ASSEMBLY TO BE LOCKED
IN PLACE.

1/8 X 1 STRAP 12" LONG

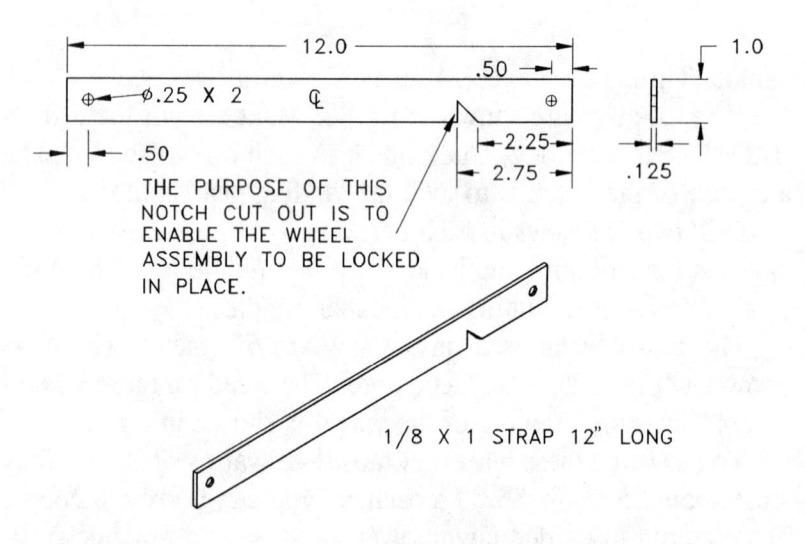

**Figure 30**     **Lock bar. Make two**

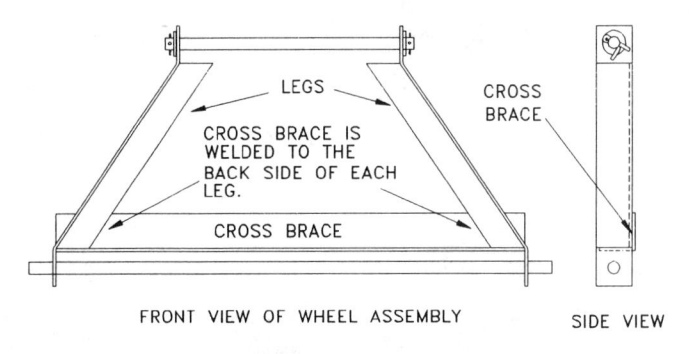

```
                    LEGS              CROSS
                                      BRACE
          CROSS BRACE IS
          WELDED TO THE
          BACK SIDE OF EACH
          LEG.

             CROSS BRACE

    FRONT VIEW OF WHEEL ASSEMBLY       SIDE VIEW
```

**Figure 31**    **Front view of landing gear**

Now that all of the parts are made for the landing gear we can begin putting it all together. Fig. 32 is a blow up of the landing gear assembly and fig. 31 is a front view. Refer to these drawings during assembly.

Bolt both hinge posts in place with 1/4-20 x 1 bolts, nuts and lock washers.

Line up the 1/2" holes in the top of each landing gear leg with the 1/2" holes in each hinge post. Slide the 1/2" hinge bar through the holes. Slide a 1/2" washer on each end of the hinge bar. To permanently hold the hinge bar in place, put a cotter pin in the 3/16" hole located on each end of the bar and bend the legs of the cotter pin back.

Set the landing gear cross brace in position as shown in fig. 31. The inside corner of the brace should fit nicely against the bottom edge of the inside angle of each leg. When the brace is in position, secure it with "C" clamps or vise grips and weld it in place.

Slide the 1/2" wheel axle through the 1/2" hole located at the bottom of each landing gear leg. Slide a wheel on each end of the axle, and then a 1/2" flat washer. To permanently hold the

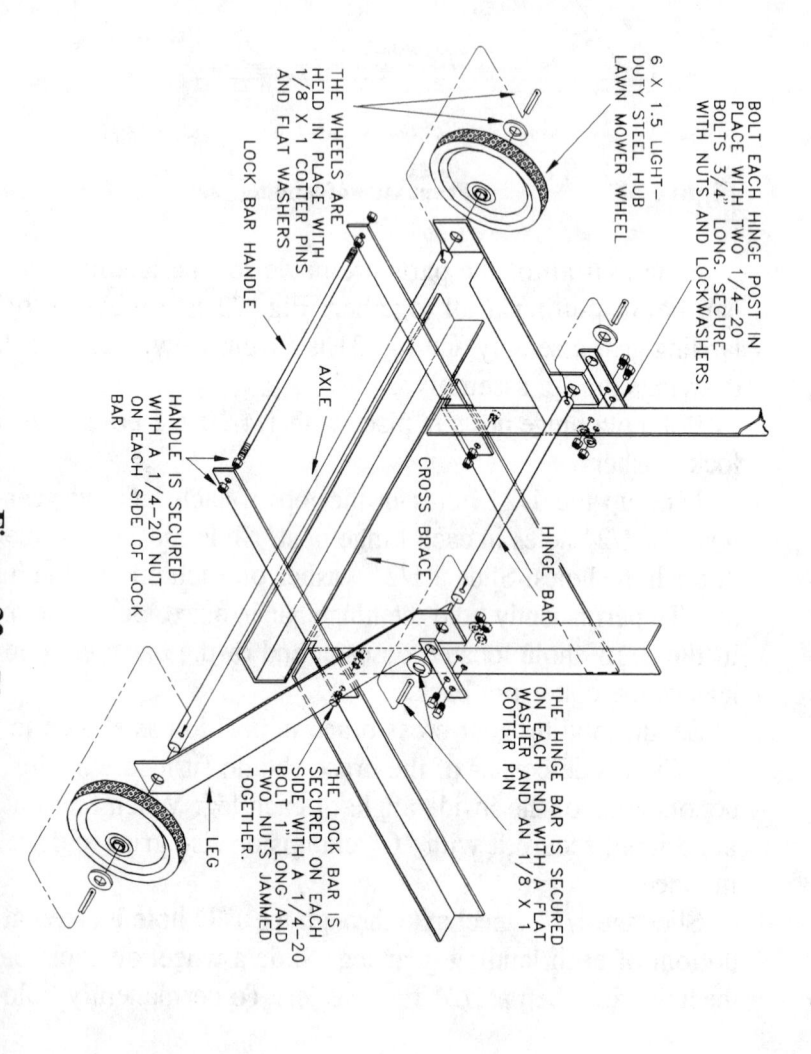

Figure 32  Blow up view of landing gear assembly

wheels in place, put a cotter pin in the 3/16" hole located at each end of the axle and bend the legs of the cotter pin back.
  Bolt a lock bar to each middle leg. See fig. 32. The notch end goes closest to the middle leg. Use 1/4-20 x 1 bolts, and secure the bolt with 2 jam nuts. Don't tighten the bolts to tight. You should be able to move the lock bars up and down easily.
  Thread a 1/4-20 nut on each end of the 1/4" round rod which is the lock bar handle. Insert one end of the handle into the 1/4" hole located at the end of one of the lock bars. Insert the other end of the handle into the other lock bar. Thread a 1/4-20 nut on each end of the handle and tighten.

**BUILDING THE VISE:** The vise design is similar to most others on the market. A screw shaft is turned causing a travel nut to move. The vise clamp is bolted to the travel nut, so when the travel nut moves so does the vise clamp. The vise clamp tightens against another stationary clamp to secure the work.
  We used a 5/8-11 x 14 right hand threaded rod for our screw shaft. The main reason for its use was its cheaper cost and ready availability. A right hand screw shaft causes the vise to work backward from other vises and it takes a little getting used to. If you have some left hand threaded rod laying around, by all means use it.

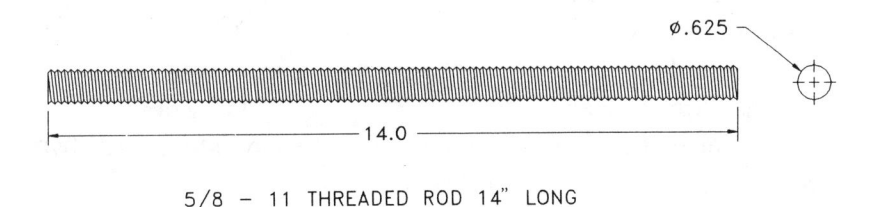

5/8 − 11 THREADED ROD 14" LONG

**Figure 33**     **Screw shaft for vise**

Cut 2 pieces of 1/4 x 1-1/2 angle 3-1/2" long for the travel nuts. Drill and tap the holes in each one as shown in fig. 34. The drill size for a hole tapped 1/2-13 is 27/64. The drill size for a hole tapped 5/8-11 is 17/32.

Make the guide plate from a piece of 1/4 x 2 flat bar 4" long. Drill two 1/2" holes at the locations shown in fig. 35. The guide plate tracks in the 2" opening down the length of the table, guiding the path of the travel nut assembly.

The top spacer plate is made from a piece of 3/8 x 3 flat bar 6" long. Drill two 3/8" holes as shown in fig. 36.

The clamp bar shown in fig. 37 is what connects the travel nut assembly to the vise clamp. Make it from a piece of 3/8 x

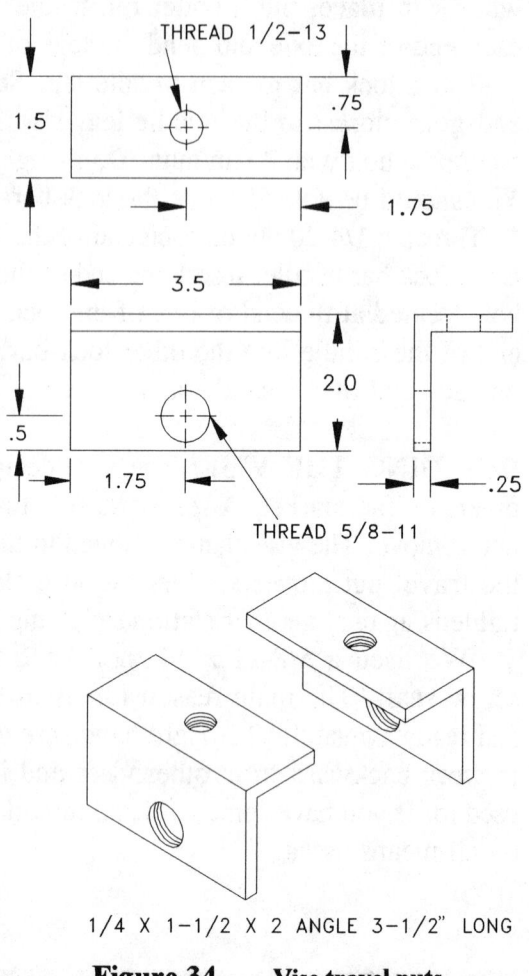

**Figure 34**  Vise travel nuts. Make two.

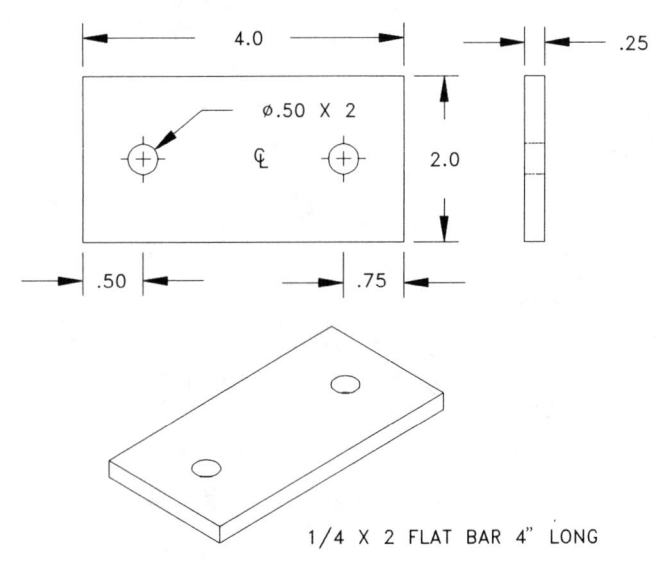

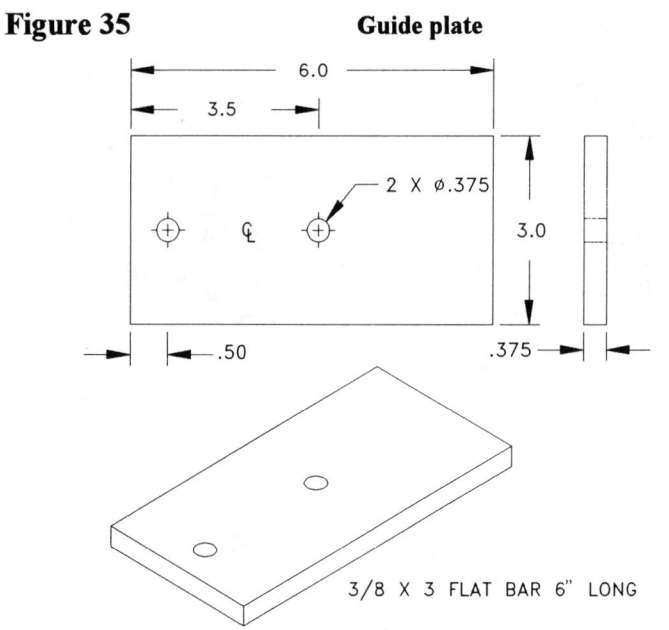

**Figure 35**    **Guide plate**

**Figure 36**    **Top spacer plate**

57

**Figure 37**     **Clamp bar**

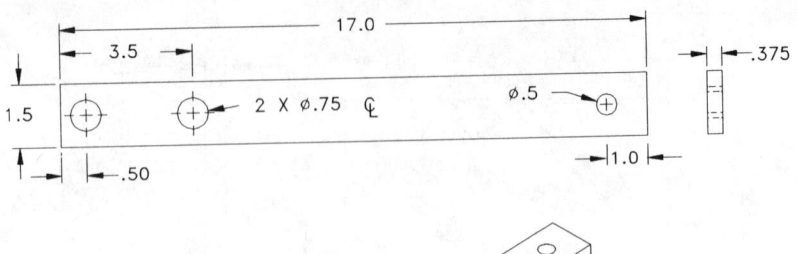

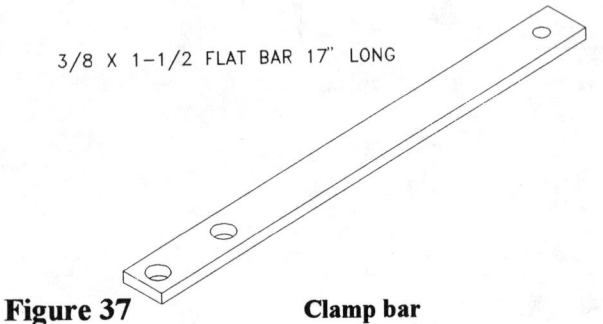

1-1/2 flat bar 17" long. Drill two 3/4" holes in one end, and a 1/2" hole in the other end at the locations shown. The 1/2" hole is used to mount the bar to the vise clamp. The two 3/4" holes are used to attach the bar to the travel nut assembly. As mentioned before, the larger holes are best step

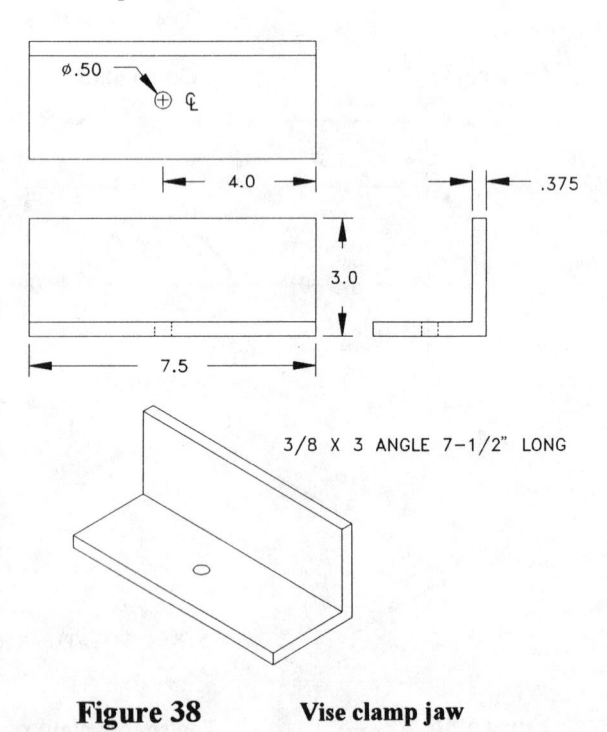

**Figure 38**     **Vise clamp jaw**

drilled on a drill press.

Cut a length of 3/8 x 3 x 3 angle 7-1/2" long for the clamp jaw. Drill a 7/16" hole at the location shown in fig. 38.

The clamp jaw guide plate is shown in fig. 39. A hole is drilled and tapped 1/2-13 at the location shown.

Cut two notches the width of a saw blade and 1/2" deep at one end of the guide plate at the location shown.

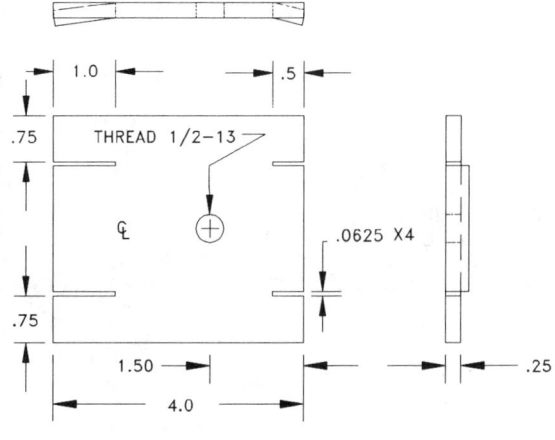

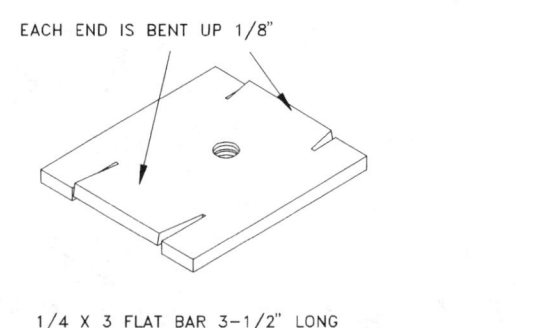

**Figure 39**  Clamp jaw guide plate

Cut two notches the width of a saw blade and 3/4" deep on the other side of the guide plate.

Bend the middle sections created by the saw cuts up about 1/8". See fig. 39. The bends are placed in the guide plate so it will track in the 2" opening down the length of the table.

A blow up drawing showing the vise assembly is shown in fig.40.

Set the guide and spacer plates on top of the saw table so they will be easy to get to. Hold one of the travel nuts under the table so the 1/2" hole lines up in the center of the 2" opening

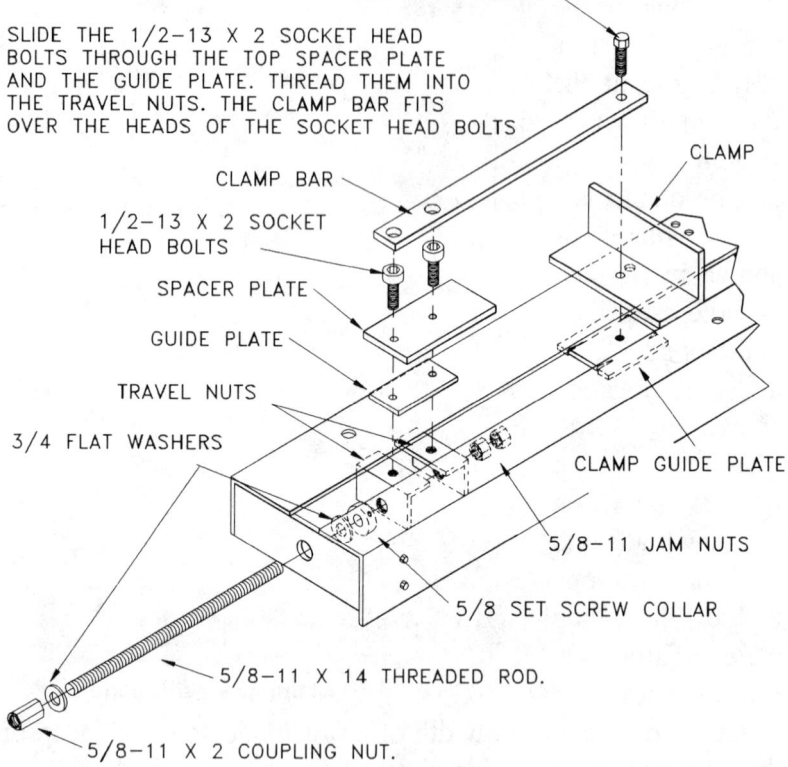

**Figure 40**  Blow up view showing the assembly

that runs down the length of the table. Grab the guide plate and set it in the opening on top of the travel nut and line the holes up. Set the spacer plate on top of the table and line up the hole in it with the hole in the guide plate and travel nut. Bolt this together with a 1/2-13 x 2 socket head bolt.

Bolt the other travel nut in place following the same

procedure.

Slide a 3/4" washer, and thread a 5/8-11 x 2 coupling nut on one end of the screw shaft. Insert the screw shaft through the 3/4" hole located at the front end of the table. Slide a 3/4" washer and a 5/8 set screw collar over the end of the shaft as it comes out of the back side of the plate. Screw the shaft through both travel nuts and slide it forward until the flat washer and coupling nut are flush against the outside of the plate.

Push the 3/4" washer and 5/8 set collar tight against the back side of the front plate and tighten the set screw

Thread two 5/8-11 nuts on the other end of the shaft located under the table. Tighten the two nuts together. Instead of the two jam nuts you could use a set screw collar. The purpose of the jam nuts is to keep the travel nuts from coming off the end of the screw shaft.

Align the two 3/4" holes in the clamp bar with the two socket head bolt heads that hold the travel nut assembly together. The holes in the bar are a little larger than the socket heads so the bar just sets in position over the socket heads.

Set the vise clamp guide plate under the saw table and in the 2" wide opening that runs down the length of the table. The bent up portions of the plate will be inside the 2" wide table opening. Set the vise jaw on top of the table and set the end of the clamp bar on top of it. Align the 1/2" hole in the clamp bar with the 1/2" hole in the vise jaw and the 1/2-13 threaded hole in the guide plate. Bolt them all together with a 1/2-13 x 2 bolt.

None of the bolts should be tightened so tight that they prevent the smooth operation of the vise, or so loose that the vise action is sloppy. If the vise jams, loosen the socket head and/or the clamp bolt until smooth operation is gained. If the action is to sloppy tighten the bolts until smooth operation is gained.

**FINISHING THE BASE SECTION OF THE SAW:** The saw table is almost done. Fig. 41 shows what the saw should look like at this point.

To make the stationary vise clamp cut a piece of 3/8 x 3 x 3 angle 9" long. Drill the two 3/8" holes in the location shown in fig. 42.

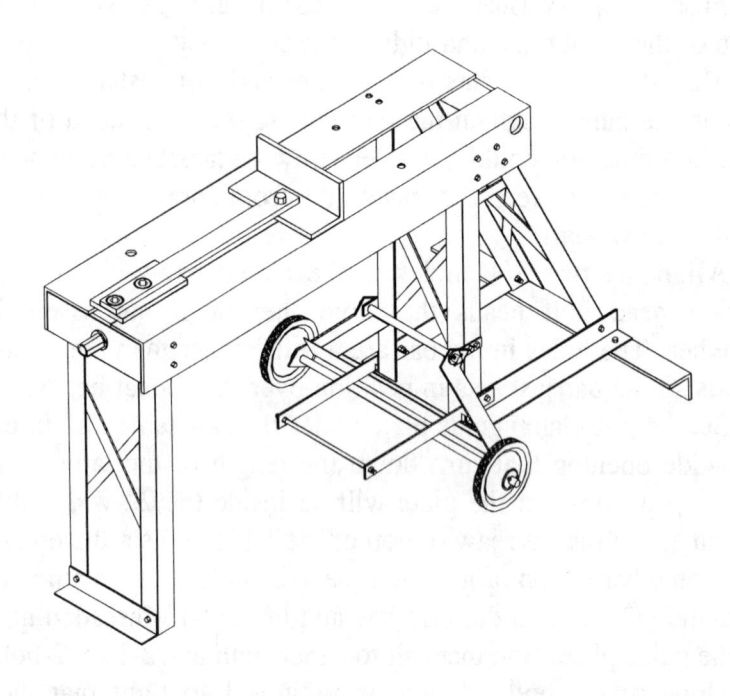

**Figure 41**      Saw table

Cut a piece of 3/8 x 1 flat bar 3-1/2" long. Drill three 1/4" holes in the locations shown in fig. 43. This is the vertical stop bracket. It determines the stop position of the vertical frame in

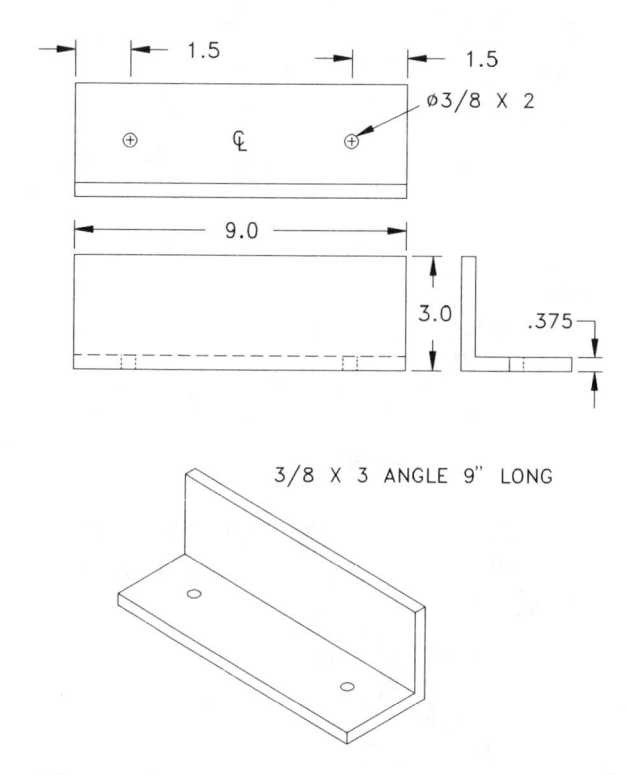

**Figure 42**  Stationary vise clamp

its upright position.

You'll need a 1/2-13 bolt 8" long with 2 nuts to serve as the horizontal stop bolt. Its purpose is to prevent the vertical frame of the saw from dropping down too far during a horizontal cut.

Fig. 44 shows the installation of the horizontal stop bolt, the vertical stop bracket and the stationary vise clamp.

To install the stop bolt, thread a nut on the end of the bolt and insert it through the 1/2" hole on the front, left side of the table top. Thread another nut on the bolt from the under side.

The height of the stop bolt is controlled by changing the position of the nuts on the bolt. When the proper height is found

TAP 1/4-20

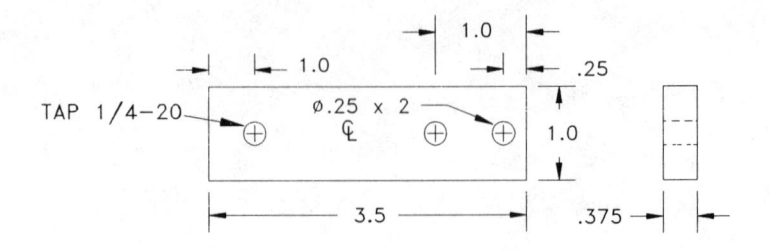

∅.25 x 2 ℄

3/8 X 1 FLAT BAR 3-1/2" LONG

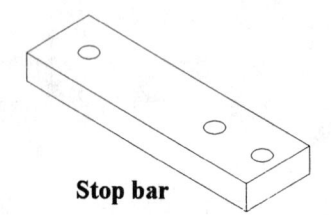

**Figure 43**  **Stop bar**

THE STATIONARY VISE CLAMP IS BOLTED ON WITH TWO 3/8-16 X 2 BOLTS, NUTS AND LOCK WASHERS.

THE STOP BAR IS BOLTED ON WITH TWO 1/4-20 X 1-1/2 BOLTS, NUTS AND LOCK WASHERS.

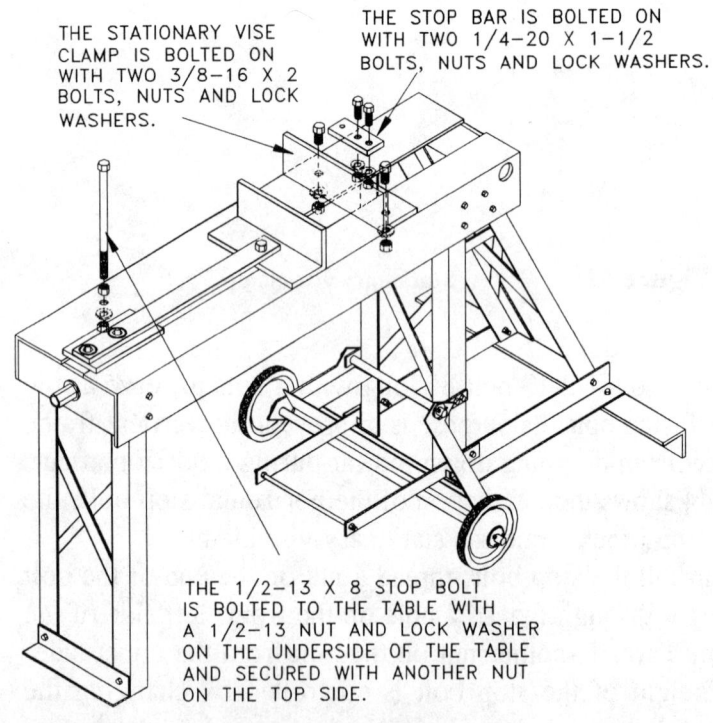

THE 1/2-13 X 8 STOP BOLT IS BOLTED TO THE TABLE WITH A 1/2-13 NUT AND LOCK WASHER ON THE UNDERSIDE OF THE TABLE AND SECURED WITH ANOTHER NUT ON THE TOP SIDE.

**Figure 44**  **Installing the stop bolt, stop bar and vise clamp**

tighten both nuts against the top of the table.

Bolt the stationary vise clamp to the table top with two 3/8-16 x 2 bolts, nuts and lock washers.

Bolt the stop bar in place with two 1/4-20 x 1-1/2 bolts, nuts and lock washers.

This completes the construction of the saw base. In the next section we will cover the construction of the vertical frame.

## SECTION 2
## THE VERTICAL FRAME ASSEMBLY

Fig. 45 shows what the saw looks like up to this point. The

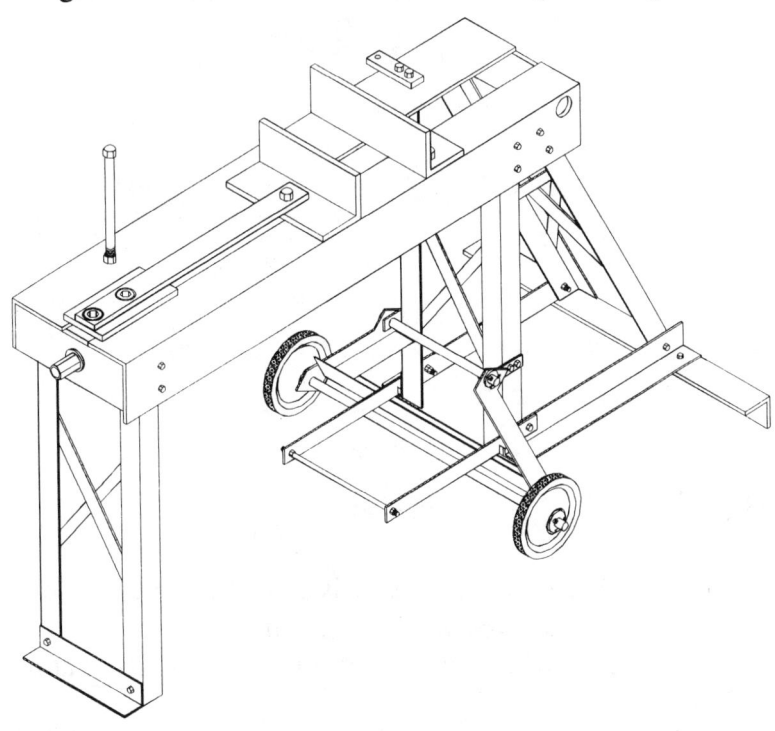

**Figure 45**          The base complete

65

purpose of the base is to hold and support the vertical frame and to hold the work to be cut, but the vertical section of the saw were getting ready to build really does most of the work. It contains the motor, the drive assembly, the blade wheels and the blade itself.

The base and the vertical frame of the saw are held together by the hinge pin. The hinge pin is shown in fig. 46. Make it from a piece of 7/8" round mild steel rod 14-1/4" long .

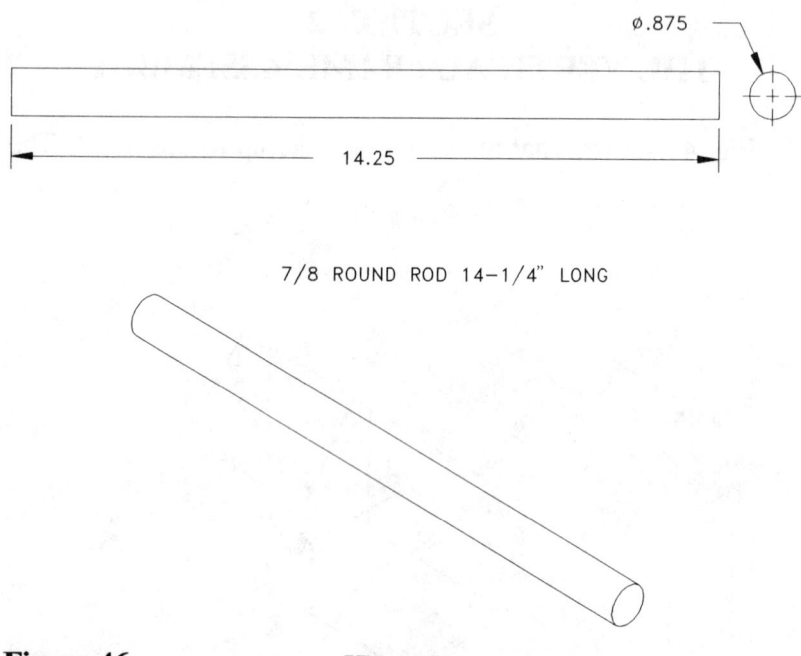

⌀.875

14.25

7/8 ROUND ROD 14−1/4" LONG

**Figure 46**     **Hinge pin**

The vertical section of the saw is connected to the base by two pivot arms that pivot on the hinge pin.

Make the left pivot arm by cutting a piece of 3/8 x 2 flat bar 25" long.

Step drill the 7/8" hole in the location shown in fig. 47. The pivot hinge fits in this hole. Also drill three 3/8" holes in the pivot arm. The two 3/8 holes at one end are for mounting the pivot arm to the vertical frame. The 3/8 tapped hole is for mounting the feed pressure control spring.

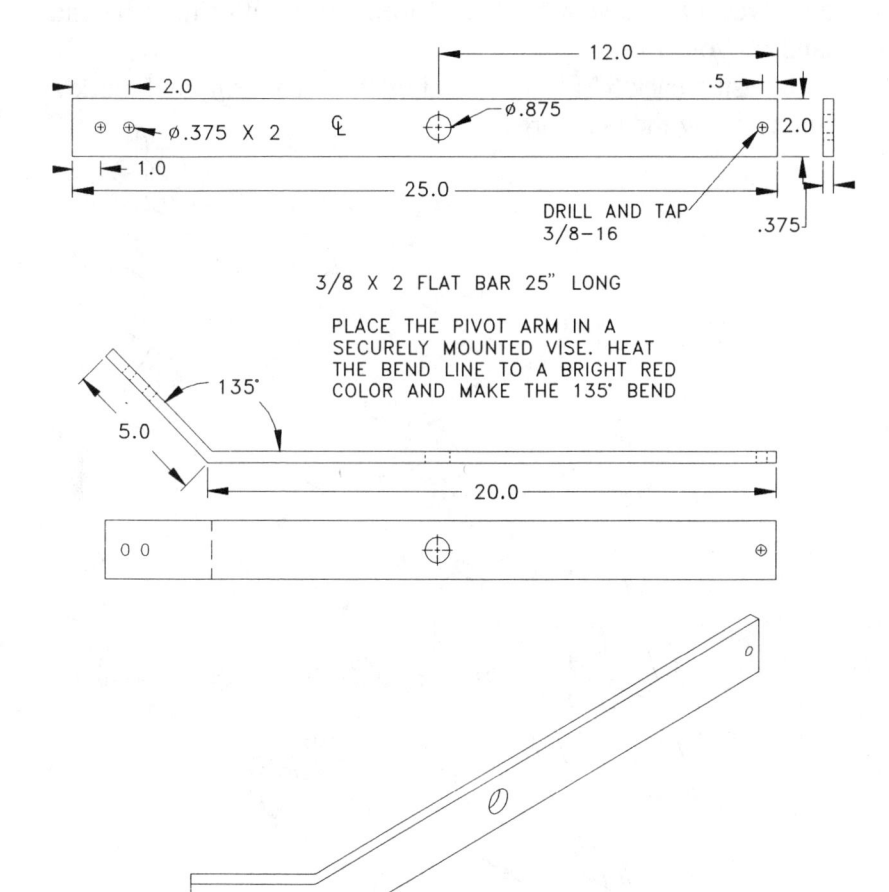

3/8 X 2 FLAT BAR 25" LONG

PLACE THE PIVOT ARM IN A SECURELY MOUNTED VISE. HEAT THE BEND LINE TO A BRIGHT RED COLOR AND MAKE THE 135° BEND

**Figure 47**     **The left side pivot arm**

As you can see in fig. 47, it is necessary to put a 135 degree bend in one end of the pivot arm. To make the bend you will need a vise that is mounted securely to a heavy bench, preferably a bench that is bolted to the floor. You don't want the leverage used to make the bend to cause the workbench to turn over, or to have a hot bar of iron come out of the vise and land on your toe.

Measure back 5" from the end of the pivot arm, and mark a line to show the bend area.

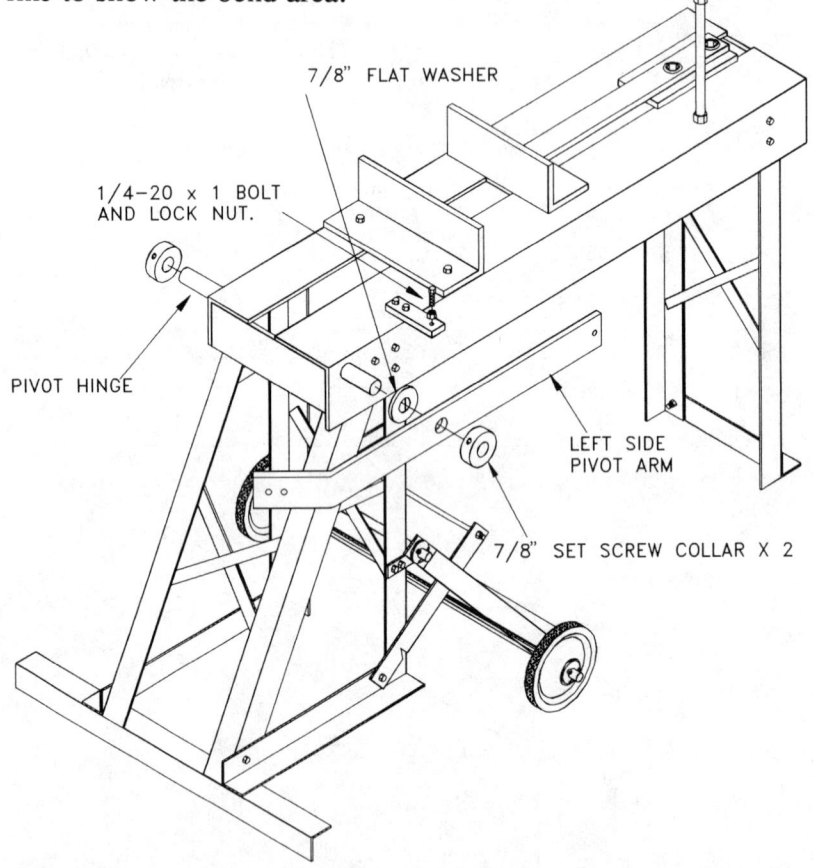

**Figure 48** Inserting the hinge pin and mounting the left side pivot arm

You will need a large crescent wrench with the jaws adjusted to fit the 3/8" thickness of the flat bar to aid in making the bend. This will keep you from having to touch the hot metal and also add some leverage to the job.

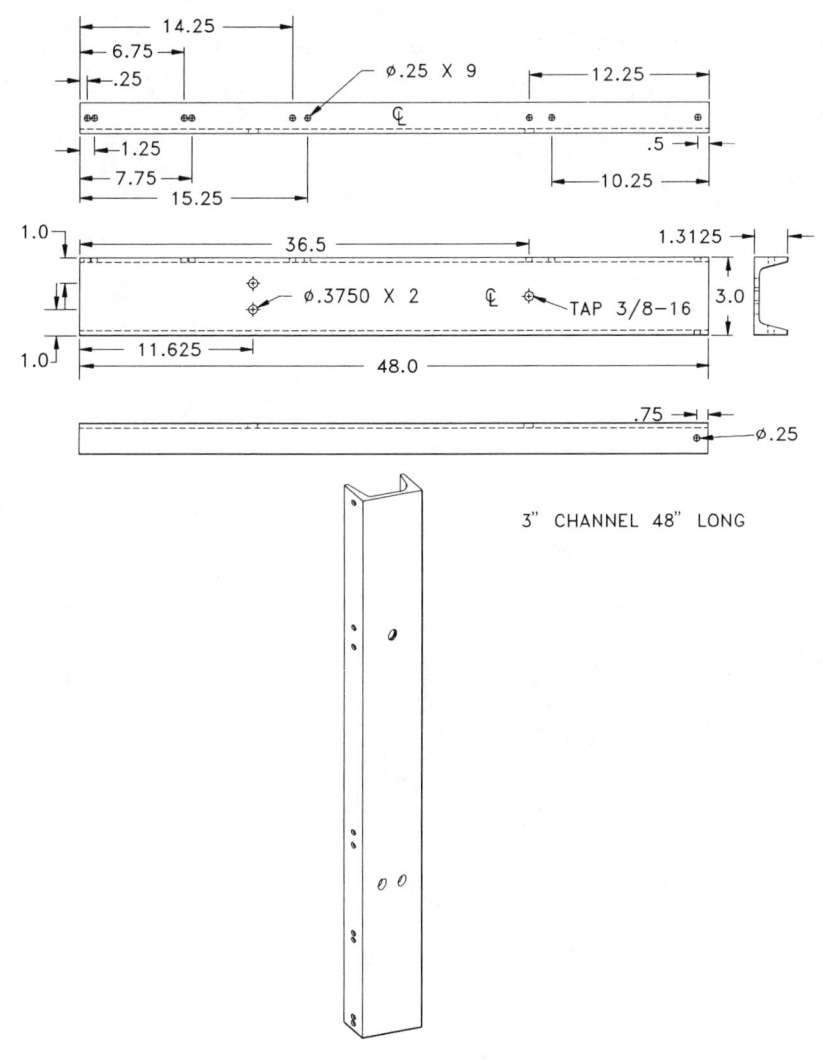

**Figure 49**  Vertical post

Look at fig. 47 and try to gain a mental vision of how far to make the bend before you apply the heat. Set a protractor to 135 degrees and place it beside the work. When you have gained a good idea of what the bend should look like remove the protractor.

Use a torch to heat the bend line to a bright red. Remember to wear eye protection and take the other necessary safety and

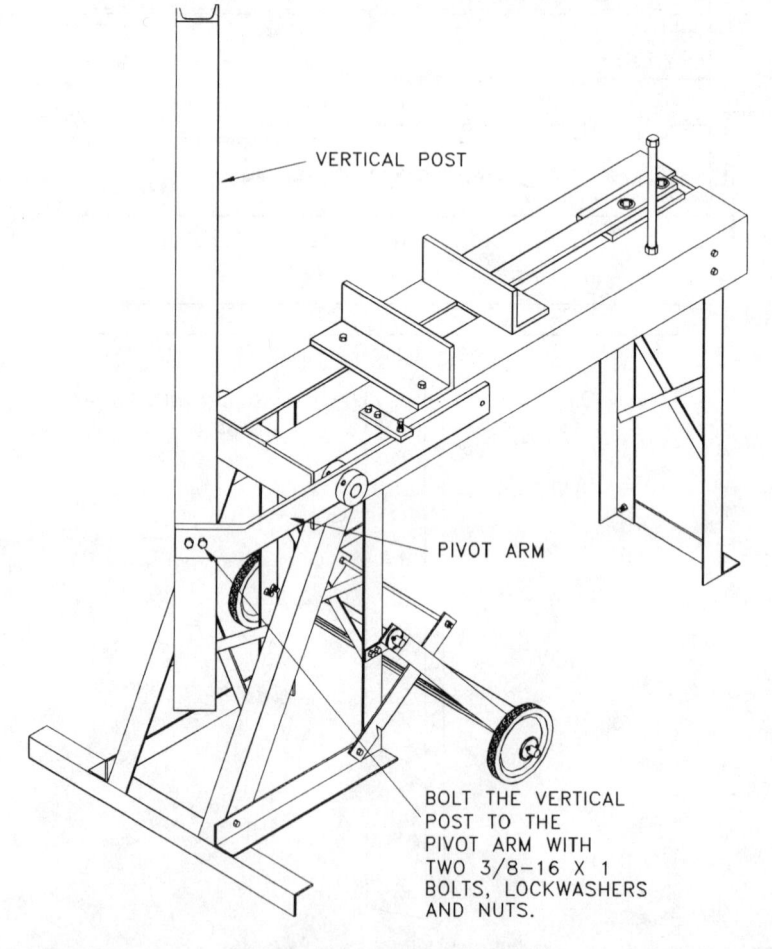

**Figure 50**     **Bolting the vertical post to the pivot arm**

fire precautions when using a torch.

The metal will be very hot and you won't want to touch it, so place the end of the crescent wrench on the end of the bar and make the approximate bend.

After the work has cooled, check the angle with the protractor. If the bend is to great, place the pivot arm on a solid surface such as an anvil and hit the back of the bend with a heavy hammer. Make sure you are wearing safety glasses.

If the bend is short repeat the heating and bending process.

Refer to fig. 48 as you perform the next few steps. Insert the

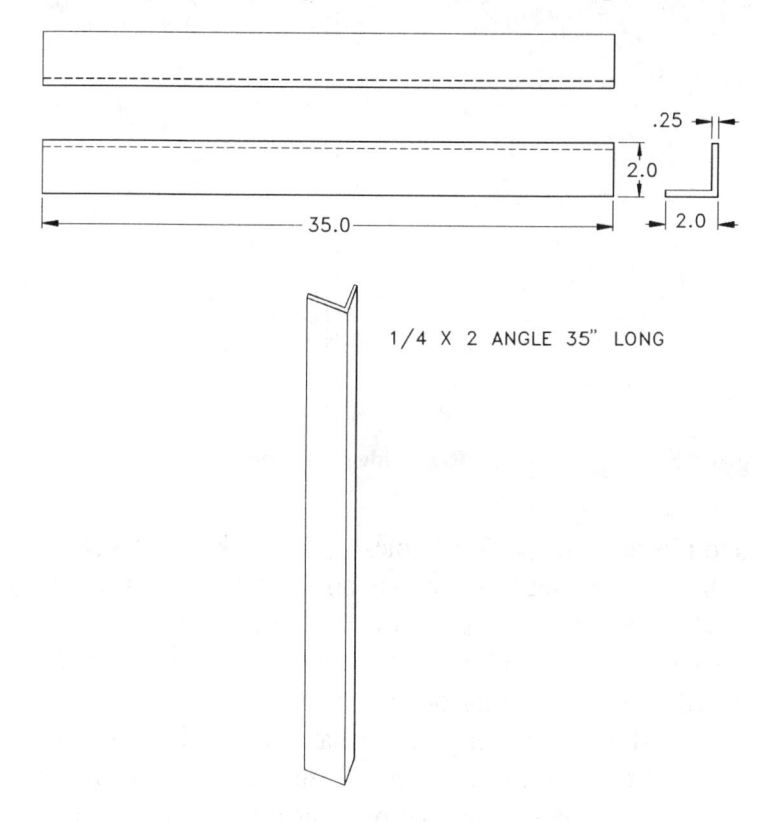

1/4 X 2 ANGLE 35" LONG

**Figure 51**     Brace for the vertical post brace

**Figure 52**      **Right side pivot arm**

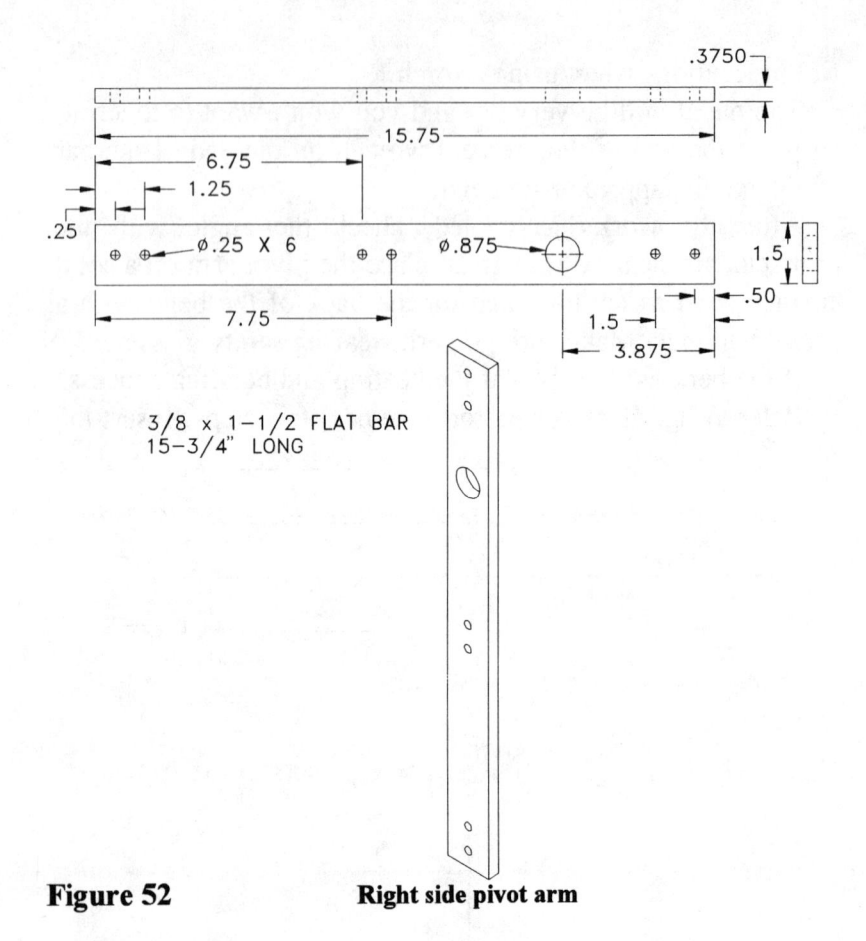

hinge pin through the 7/8" holes at the back of the saw base.

Place a 7/8" set screw collar on the right side of the hinge pin. Place a 7/8" flat washer on the left side of the hinge pin. Place the left side pivot arm on the left side of the pivot hinge, and 7/8" set screw collar on after that.

Align the outside set screw collar flush with the end of the hinge and tighten the set screw. Push the hinge in so that the inside 7/8" flat washer and the pivot arm are flush against each other, and the side of the table.

Push the set screw collar on the right side flush against the table and tighten the set screw.

Just in case I haven't mentioned it before, the left and right

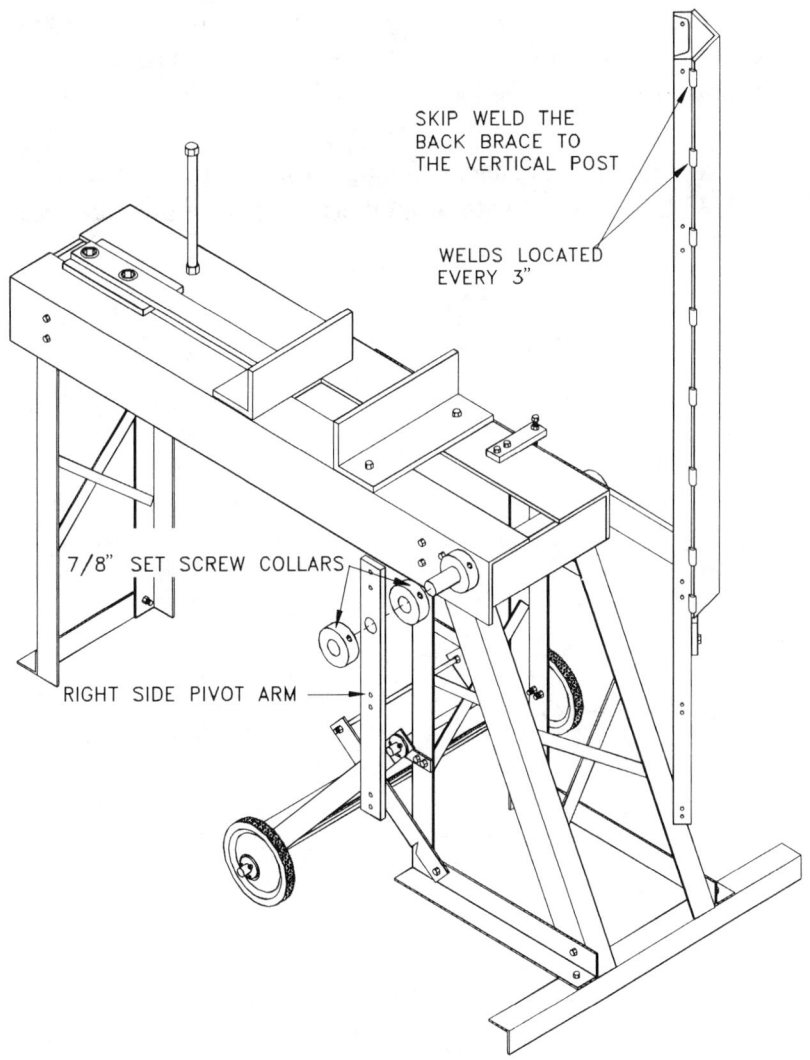

**Figure 53**     Welding the vertical post brace and attaching the right side pivot arm

side of the saw are determined when you are facing the front of the saw. The front end is the end that controls the vise.

Put the 1/4-20 x 1-1/2 bolt and nut into the vertical stop bar as shown in fig. 48. Adjusting the bolt up or down will determine the position of the vertical frame. When the proper level position is found the locknut is tightened securing the stop bolt.

Cut a piece of 3" channel 48" long for the vertical post. Drill nine 1/4" holes in one side of the vertical post in the locations

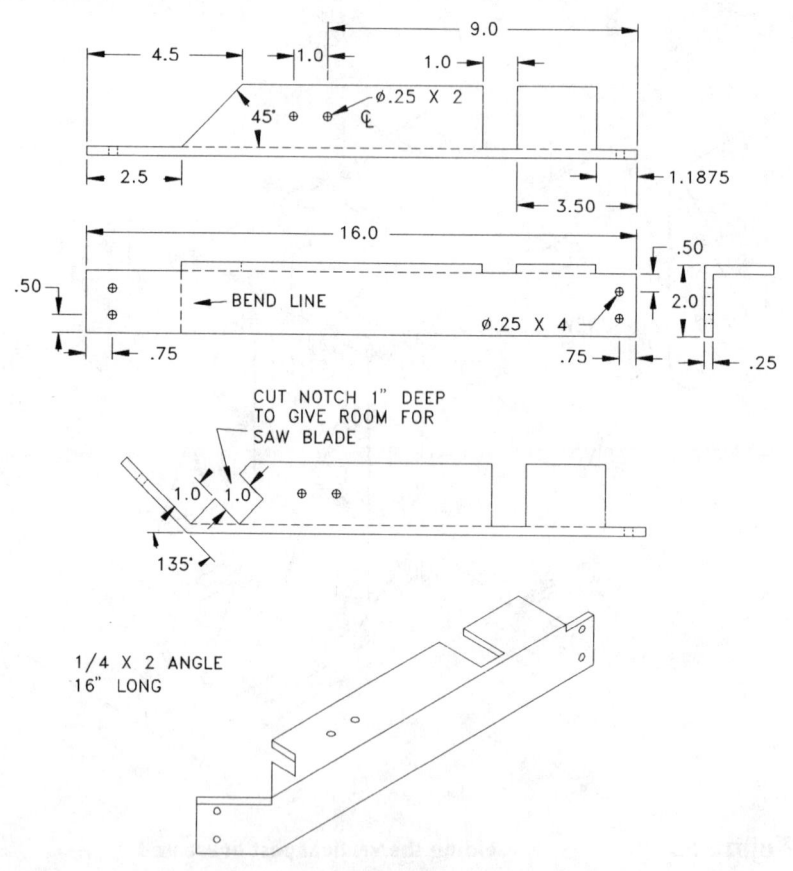

**Figure 54**      **Lower section top cross brace**

shown in fig 49. Six of the holes are for mounting the lower frame rails. The other three holes are for mounting the upper frame rails

Drill one 1/4" hole in the other side of the vertical post. This hole is for the upper frame rail.

Drill two 3/8" holes in the back of the vertical post and drill and tap 1 hole 3/8-16. The left side pivot arm mounts to the two 3/8" holes and the inside upper frame brace mounts in the tapped hole.

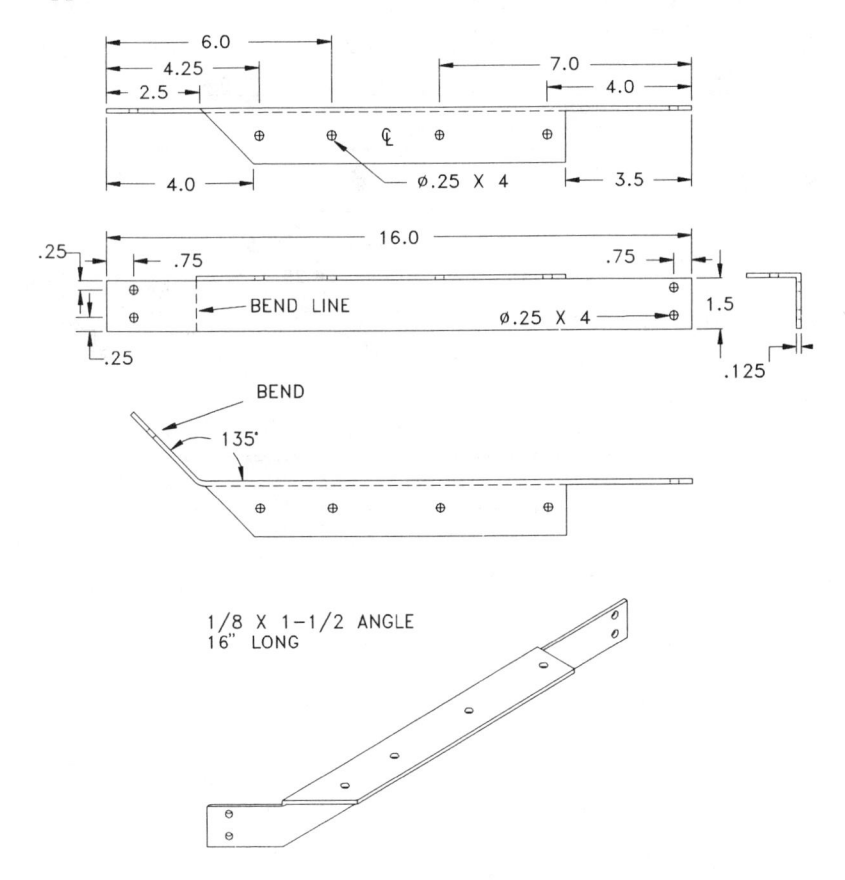

**Figure 55**     Lower section, middle cross brace

75

Mount the vertical post to the left side pivot arm by lining the two 3/8" holes in the vertical post with the two 3/8" holes in the left side pivot arm. Bolt the two together with two 3/8-16 x 1 bolts and secure with nuts and lock washers. See fig. 50.

Make the back brace for the vertical post by cutting a length of 1/4 x 2 angle 35" long. This is the vertical post brace and it is shown in fig. 51.

Set the vertical post brace on the back of the vertical post. Align the top edge of the brace with the top edge of the post.

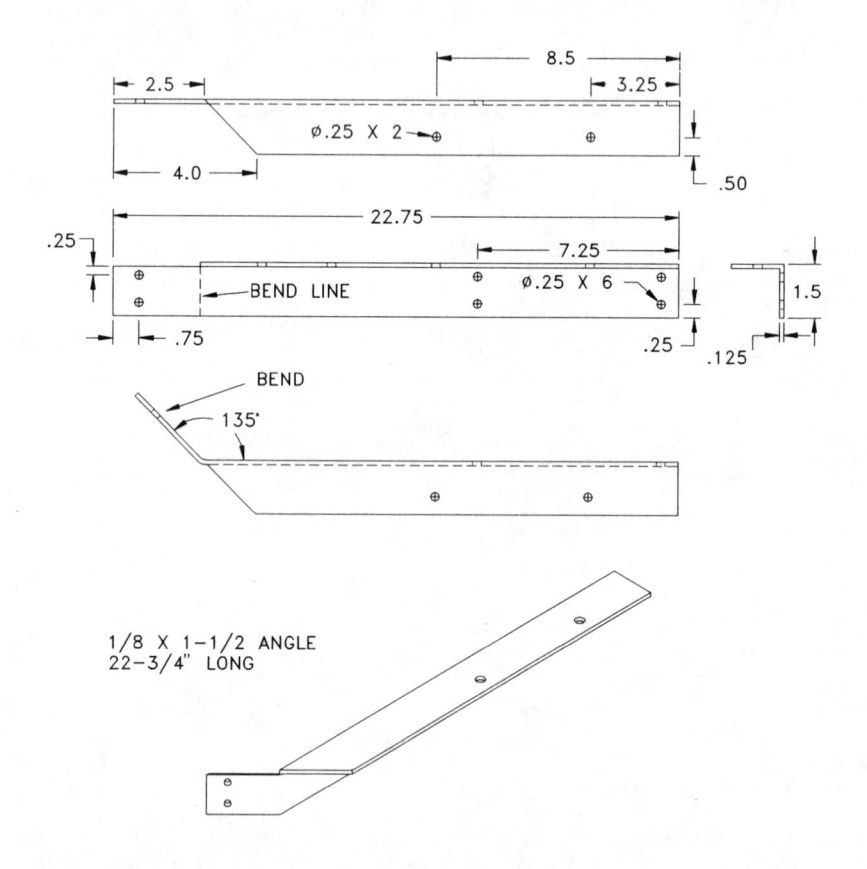

**Figure 56**           **Inside frame rail**

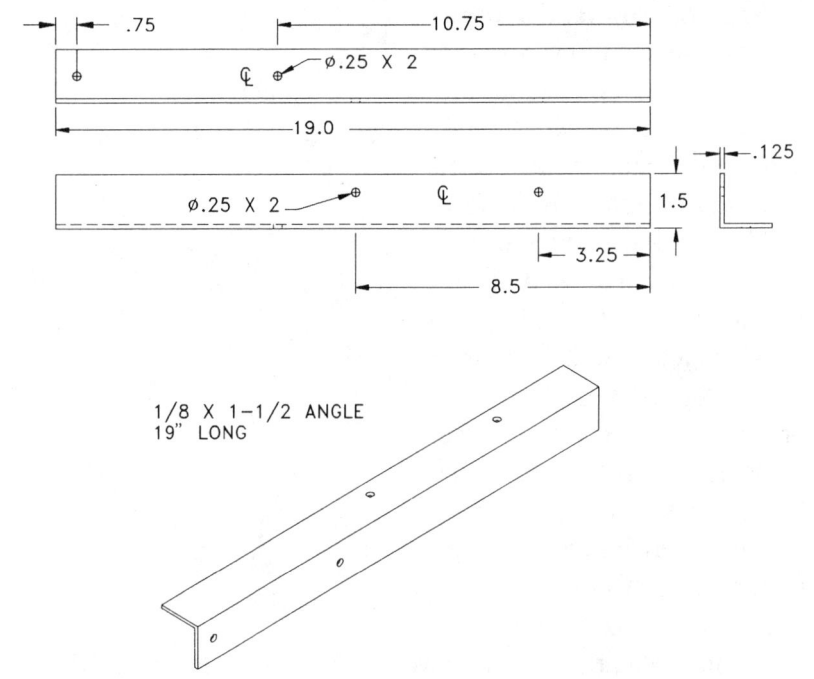

**Figure 57**     Outside frame rail for the drive frame

The bottom edge of the brace should be just above the left side pivot arm. The side edges of the brace and post will line up nicely. Clamp both pieces together with "C" clamps.

Weld the brace to the post at 3" intervals. Tack weld both sides at each end first. Then begin welding at the center and alternate towards each end from front to back as you go. A full weld is not necessary and doing so would cause the post to warp. A 1/2" weld on both sides at 3" intervals will give all the strength necessary.

There are three cross braces in the lower frame that connect the vertical post to the right side pivot arm. These cross braces have other purposes as well and we will discuss them as we build each brace.

Fig. 60 shows the cross braces bolted in position and may help you understand the purpose of the holes, cutouts and bends made in each one.

Study figure 54 before making the lower section, top brace. Then cut a piece of 1/4 x 2 angle 16" long.

Make the 3 cut outs shown in the top view of the cross brace. The cut out on the right is 1-3/16" wide. The purpose is to leave an opening for the cross brace to mount to the vertical post. The cut out next to it is 1" wide and is for blade clearance. The third cut out on the left side allows clearance for mounting the brace to the right side pivot arm.

Drill the two 1/4" holes shown in the top view. The lower blade guide assembly will mount here.

Now, looking at the side view in fig. 54, drill the two 1/4" holes on each end of the cross brace. These are mounting holes.

To avoid confusion it was necessary to show two top views in fig. 54. Make the 1" wide cut out shown in the second top view to give clearance for the saw blade. Also make the 135 degree bend as shown. The same methods are used to make this bend as were used to bend the pivot arm.

The middle cross brace is shown in fig. 55. Make it from a piece of 1/8 x 1-1/2 angle 16" long. The top view shows the two cut outs, one on each end.

Drill the four 1/4" holes in the top as shown. The two outside holes are for mounting the drive assembly cross brace.

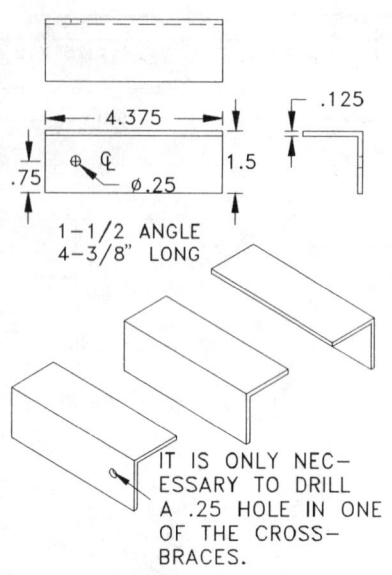

**Figure 58**  Cross braces

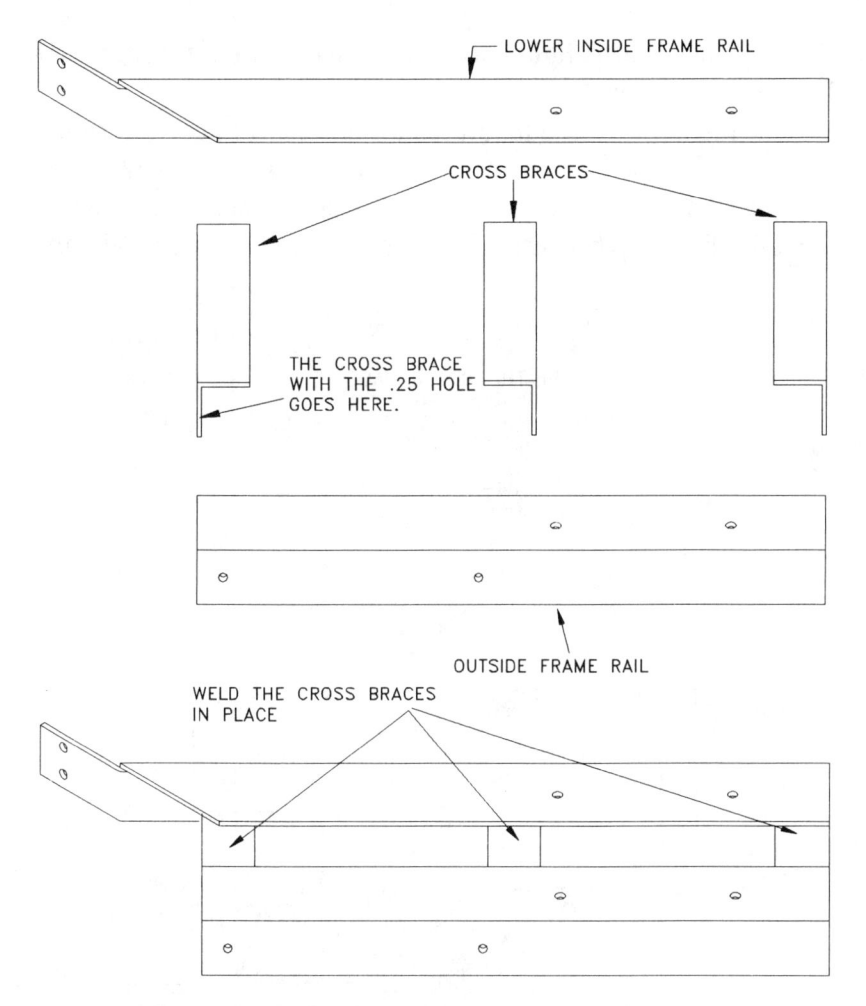

**Figure 59**  **The lower section bottom cross brace assembly**

A pillow block bearing will be mounted to the two inside holes.

Referring to the side view, drill the four 1/4" mounting holes. The two on the right are used for mounting the brace to the vertical post. The two on the left are for mounting the brace to the right side pivot arm.

Make the 135 degree bend as shown in the second top view.

The 1/8" material is light enough so it will not be necessary to heat the bend area.

Bolt the top and middle braces to the vertical post and right side pivot arm as shown in fig. 60. Use 1/4-20 x 1-1/2 bolts with nuts and lock washers. There may be a problem here with the holes lining up because of differences in the angle bends on

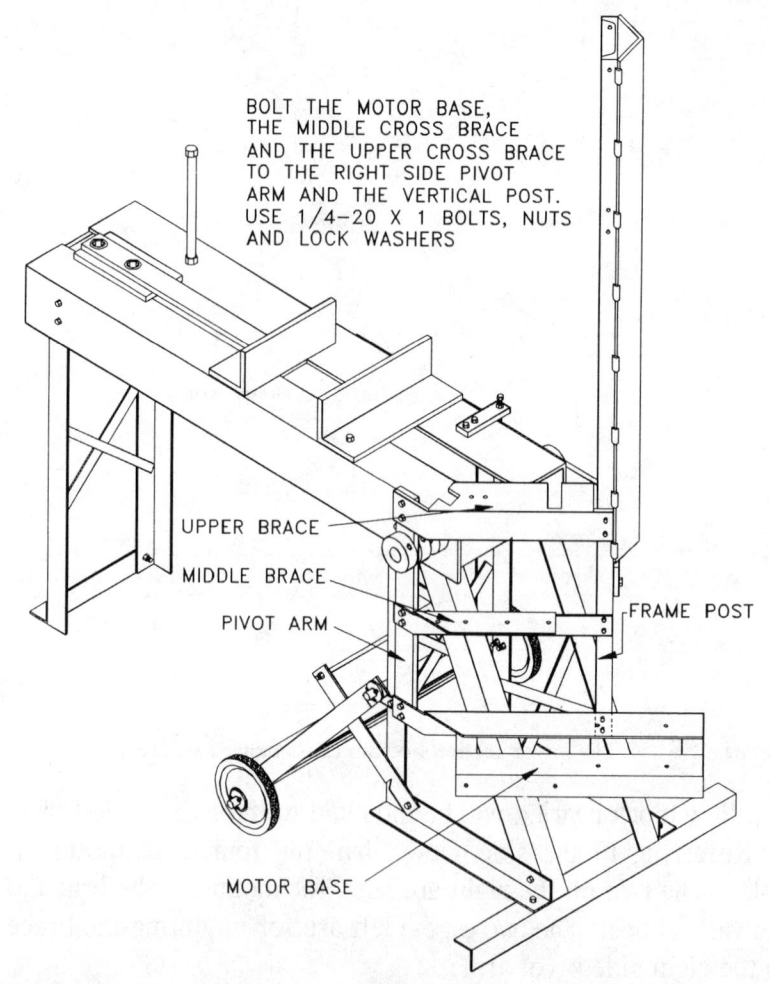

**Figure 60** Mounting the top, middle and bottom cross braces

the pivot arm, or the braces themselves. This is not a serious problem, but it may be necessary to redrill the holes to compensate.

The lower section bottom cross brace is built as an assembly. Fig. 59 shows the individual parts of the completed assembly.

The first part to make is the inside frame rail shown in fig. 56. Cut a piece of 1/8 x 1-1/2 angle 22-3/4" long. Drill the two 1/4" holes shown in the top view, and the six 1/4" holes shown in the side view. Make the 135 degree bend as shown in the second top view in fig.56.

The outside frame rail is shown in fig 57. It is made from 1/8 x 1-1/2 angle 19" long. Drill the two 1/4" holes in the locations shown in the top view and drill two 1/4" holes shown in the side view.

There are three cross braces to make and they are shown in fig. 58. Cut three pieces of 1/8 x 1-1/2 angle 4-3/8" long. Two of the braces are left blank, but drill a hole in the third one at the location shown in fig. 58.

Weld the cross braces in position between the inside and outside frame rails as shown in fig. 59.

Bolt the completed lower frame rail assembly to the vertical post and the right side pivot arm as shown in fig 60. As explained earlier, if the mounting holes do not line up it may be necessary to relocate them.

**THE COUNTER SHAFT STAND & MOTOR MOUNT:** The counter shaft stand holds the counter shaft and the motor mount. The motor mount holds the motor that drives the saw. They are simple to construct and are made of angle and strap iron.

The base rails are an opposing pair. To make them, cut two pieces of 1/8 x 1-1/2 angle 6-1/2" long. Drill a 1/4" hole on each end in the locations shown in fig. 61. After the holes ar drilled, cut a 1/4" wide slot on each end. The slots allow us to

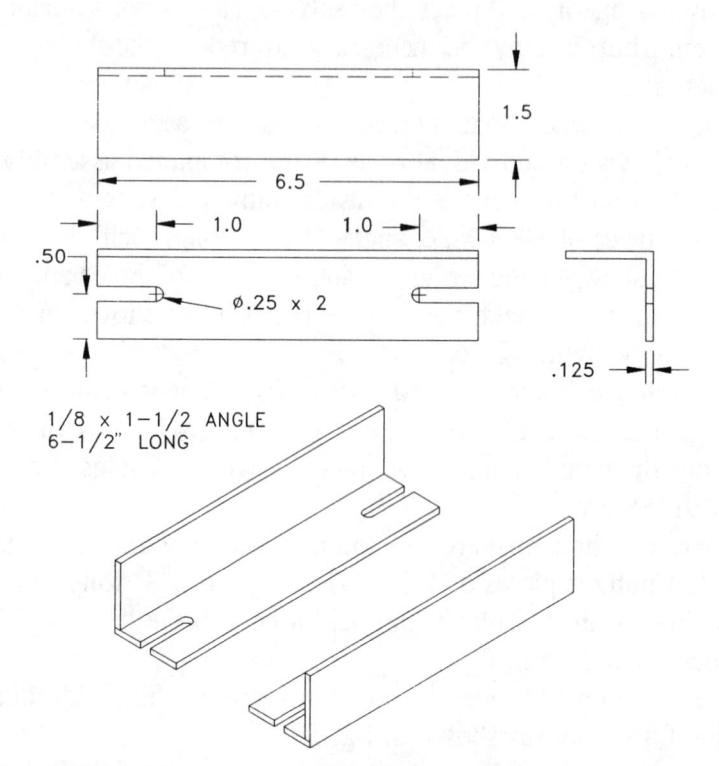

**Figure 61**      Base rails. Make an opposing pair

adjust the counter shaft stand to tighten or loosen the drive belt.

Make an opposing pair of side rails by cutting two pieces of 1/8 x 1-1/2 angle 10-1/2" long.

Drill the two 1/4" holes shown in the top view in fig. 62. The motor mount will bolt to the frame using these holes.

Drill the two 1/4" holes shown in the bottom view. The counter shaft pillow block bearings will mount using these holes.

To make the rail spreaders shown in figure 63, cut 3 pieces of 1/8 x 1 strap iron 4" long.

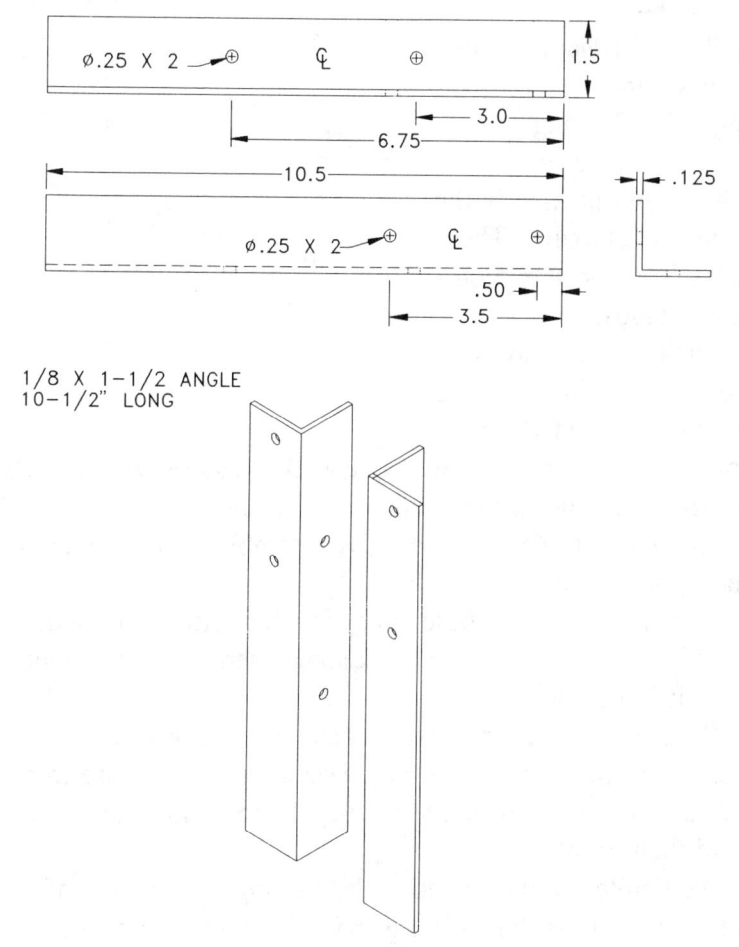

**Figure 62**  Side rails. Make an opposing pair

Drill two 1/4" holes in two of them in the locations shown. These are the motor mount spreaders. The other spreader is the base rail spreader and it does not require holes.

The motor mount rails are an opposing pair and are shown

in fig. 64.

To make them, cut two pieces of 1/8 x 1-1/2 angle 6-1/2" long.

Drill and tap two holes 1/4-20 on one side in the location shown. These holes are for the motor mount studs.

Drill two 1/4 holes on the other side in the location shown. These holes are for mounting the motor mount to the counter shaft stand.

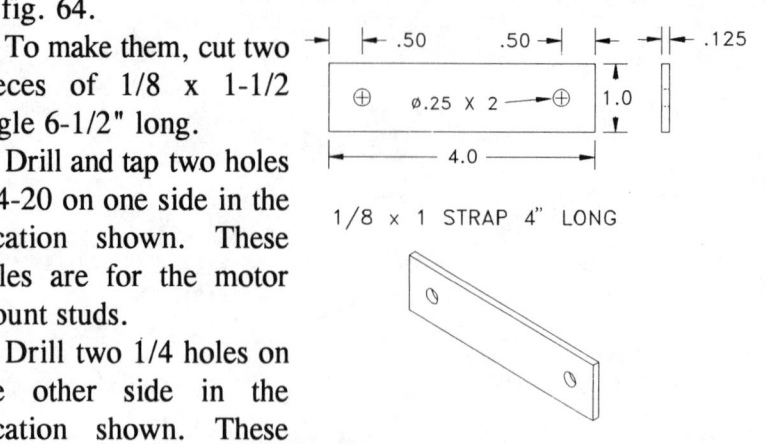

**Figure 63** Rail spreader. Make three

Refer to fig. 65 as we discuss assembling the counter shaft and motor mount.

Assemble the two base rails first by setting the blank rail spreader between them. Locate it somewhere close to center and weld it in position.

Set the base rails on a level surface and align a side rail with the rear edge of each base rail. Use a framing square to make sure that the side rails are straight. Clamp them in position and weld them in place.

Assemble the motor mount by bolting the rail spreaders to the motor rails as shown in fig. 65. The bolts will extend about 3/4" out the back of the motor mount and serve as studs for mounting the motor.

Mount the motor mount assembly to the side rails of the counter shaft stand with 1/4-20 x 1 bolts, nuts and lock washers.

After the counter shaft stand and motor mount are assembled mount them to the lower cross brace assembly on the vertical saw frame. Use 1/4-20 x 1 bolts, nuts and lock washers. Notice

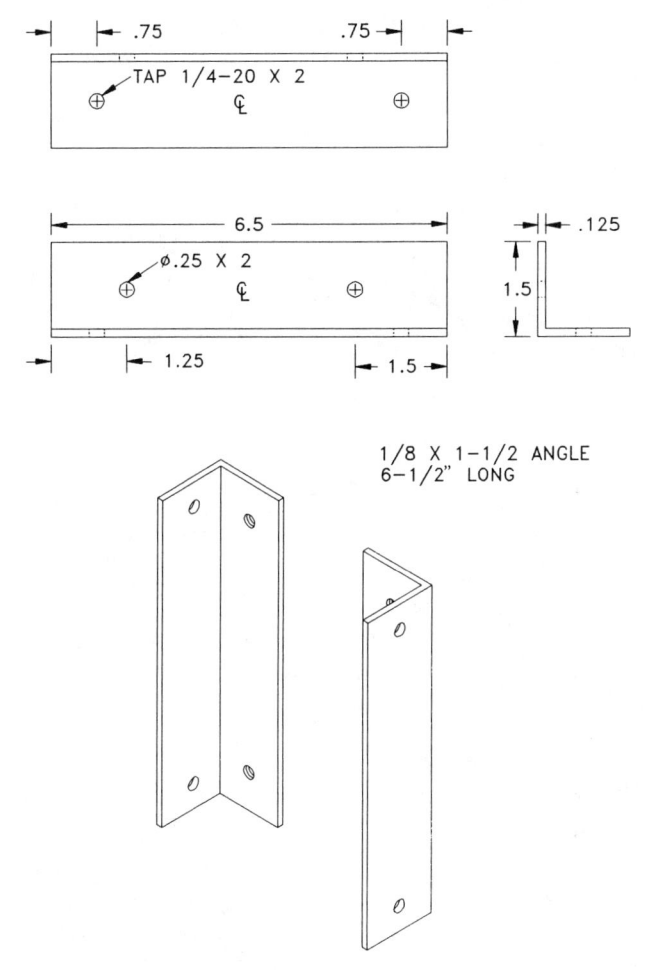

**Figure 64**  Motor mount side rails. Make an opposing pair.

how the slots in the base rails of the counter shaft stand allow it to be adjusted either forward or back. This adjustment tightens or loosens the drive belt.

85

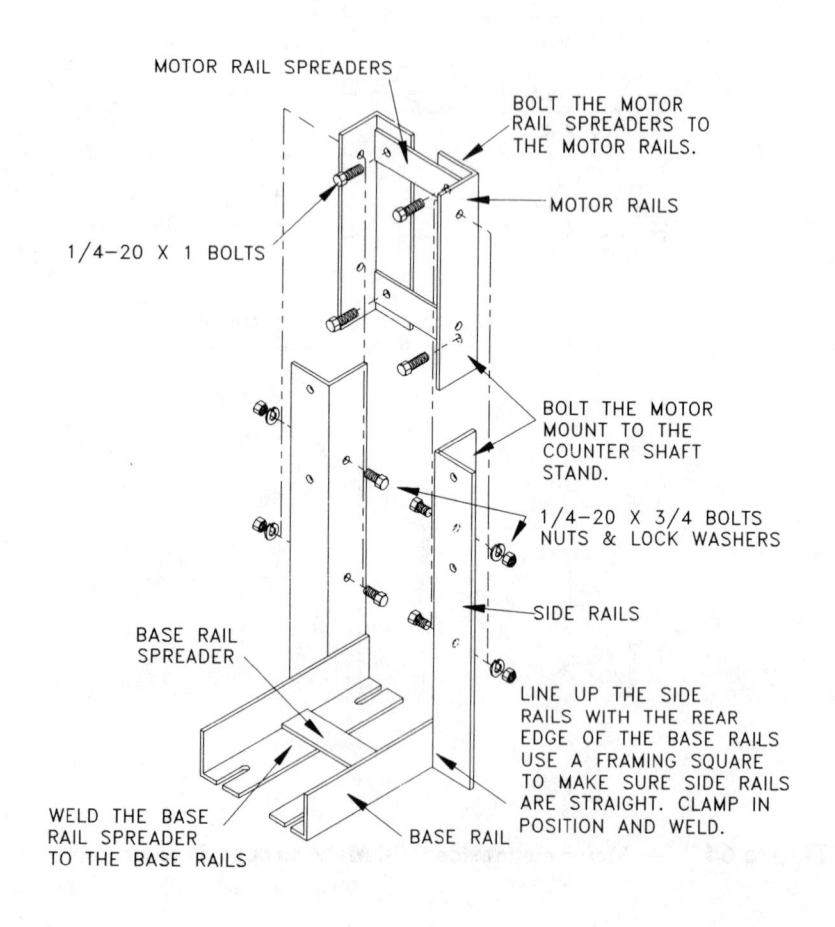

**Figure 65** Assembling the counter shaft stand and motor mount.

BOLT THE COUNTER SHAFT STAND
TO THE LOWER CROSS BRACE
ASSEMBLY WITH FOUR 1/4-20
BOLTS 1-1/2" LONG. SECURE
WITH NUTS AND LOCK WASHERS.

MOTOR MOUNT

COUNTER SHAFT STAND

LOWER CROSS BRACE ASSEMBLY.

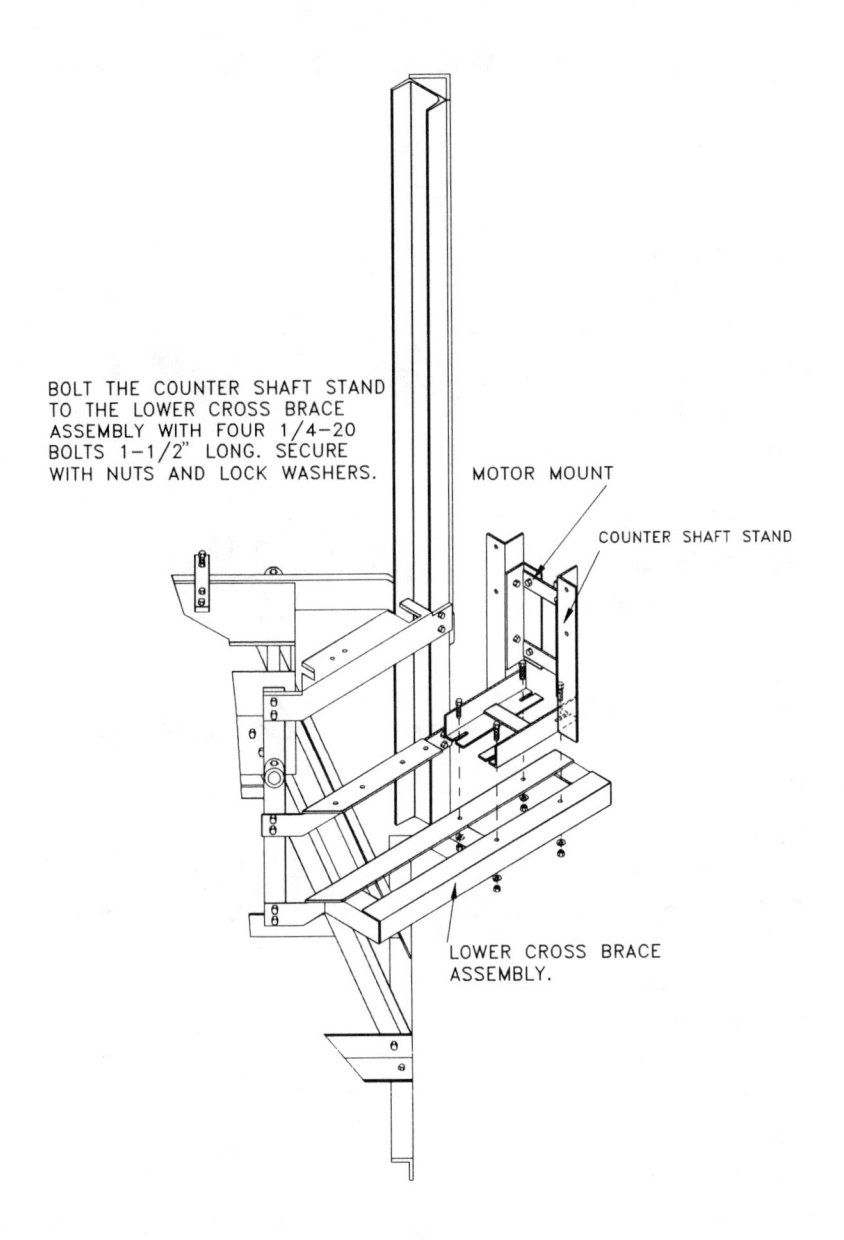

**Figure 66** Mounting the counter shaft stand and motor mount to the lower cross brace assembly on the vertical post.

## THE DRIVE SHAFT STAND

The drive shaft stand holds the pillow block bearings that support the drive shaft.

Make the left corner post by cutting a piece of 1/8 x 1-1/2 angle 8" long.

Drill the three 1/4" holes at the locations shown in fig. 67.

The right side corner post is shown in fig. 68. Make it from a piece of 3/8 x 3/4 flat bar 8" long.

Drill a 1/4" hole in each end as shown.

The drive frame cross braces are shown in fig. 69. Two are required. Make them

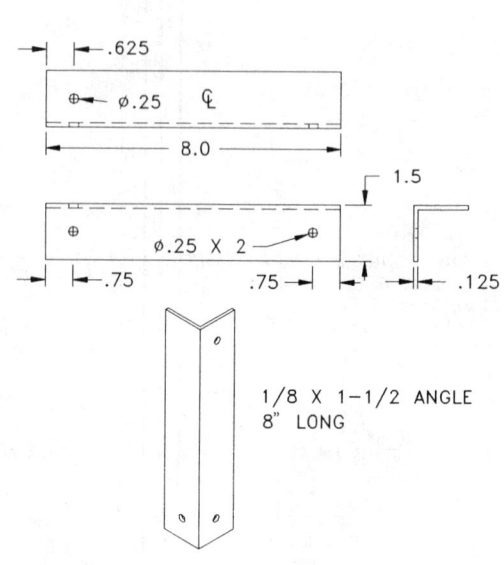

**Figure 67**   Left side corner post

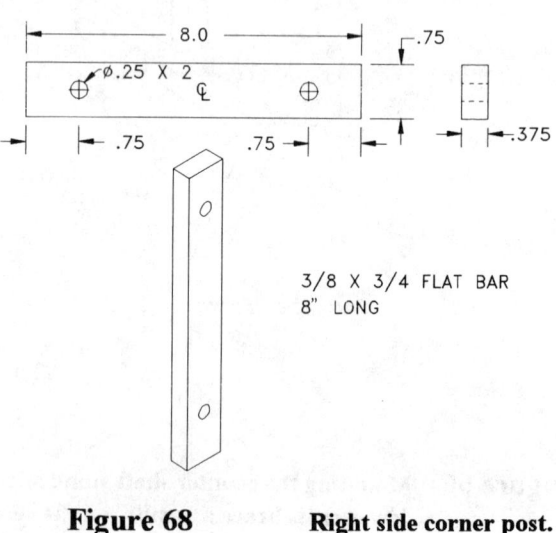

**Figure 68**   Right side corner post.

88

out of 1/4 x 3/4 flat bar 4-3/4" long. Drill a 1/4" hole in each end as shown.

Make the outer frame drive frame rail from a piece of 1/8 x 1-1/2 angle 9" long.

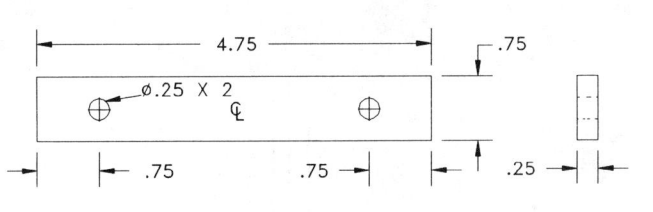

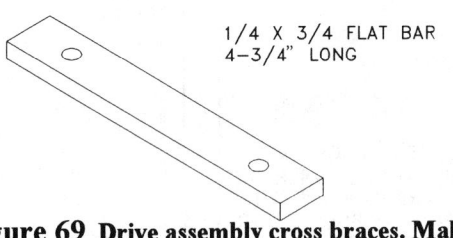

**Figure 69** Drive assembly cross braces. Make 2.

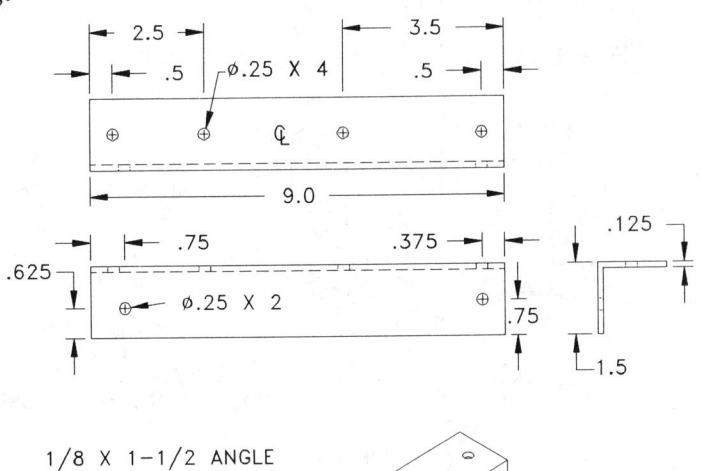

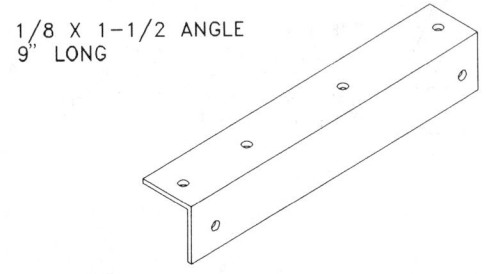

**Figure 70**   Outer drive frame rail

89

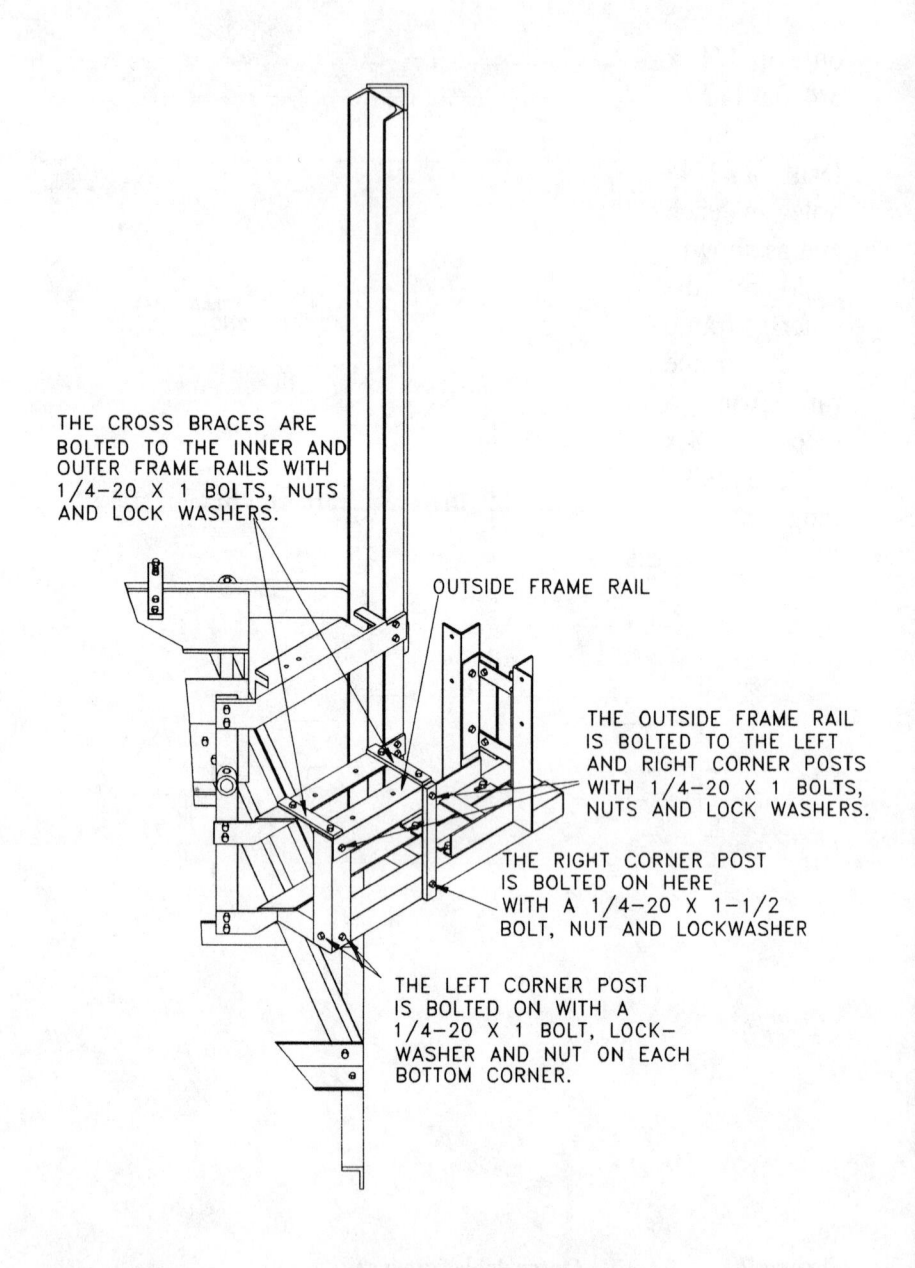

**Figure 71**     Assembling the drive shaft stand.

90

Drill the six 1/4" holes as shown in fig. 70. The two outside holes shown in the top view are for the cross braces. The two inside holes shown in the top view are for the drive shaft pillow block bearing. The two holes drilled in the side are for mounting the left and right side corner posts.

Assemble the drive shaft stand as shown in fig. 71. All assembly is done with 1/4-20 x 1 bolts, nuts and lock washers.

**THE UPPER VERTICAL FRAME ASSEMBLY:** The blade wheel is enclosed by the upper vertical frame assembly. The adjustable upper blade guide rollers also mount to the upper frame as do the bearings and shaft for the upper blade wheel.

Begin making the vertical frame by first making the inside bottom brace. Cut a piece of 3/8 x 2 flat bar 13-1/2" long. Cut two notches out of the brace in the locations shown in fig. 72.

THE NOTCHES ARE CUT FOR BLADE CLEARANCE

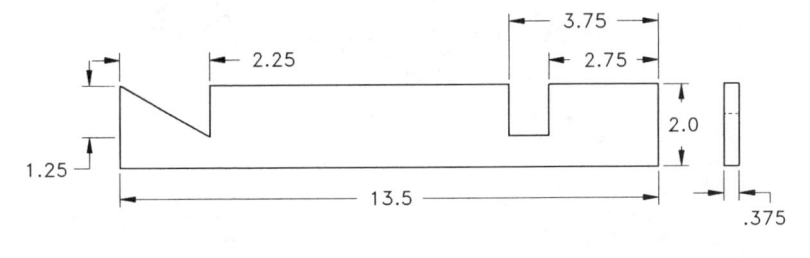

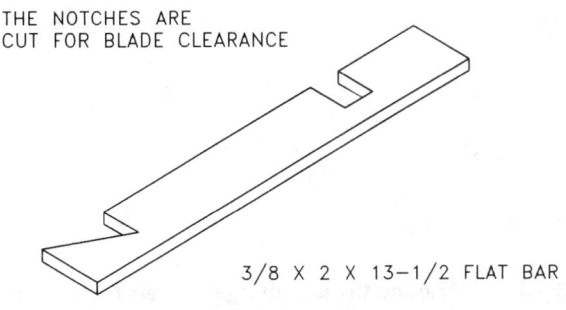

3/8 X 2 X 13-1/2 FLAT BAR

**Figure 72** Inside bottom brace for the upper vertical frame assembly

The notches are for blade clearance.

Make two mounting brackets for the bottom brace out of 1/8 x 1 angle 2" long.

Drill two 1/4" holes in one of the brackets as shown in fig. 73. Drill a 3/8" hole in the other one where shown.

Weld the mounting brackets we just made to each end of the bottom brace. The bracket with the single 3/8" hole goes to the back of the brace and the one with the two 1/4" holes goes to the front of the brace.

Cut a piece of 1/4 x 1-1/2 angle 14" long for the right side upper frame rail. See fig. 74 for the hole locations in the right side frame rail.

Drill and tap a 1/4-20 hole in the top of the frame rail

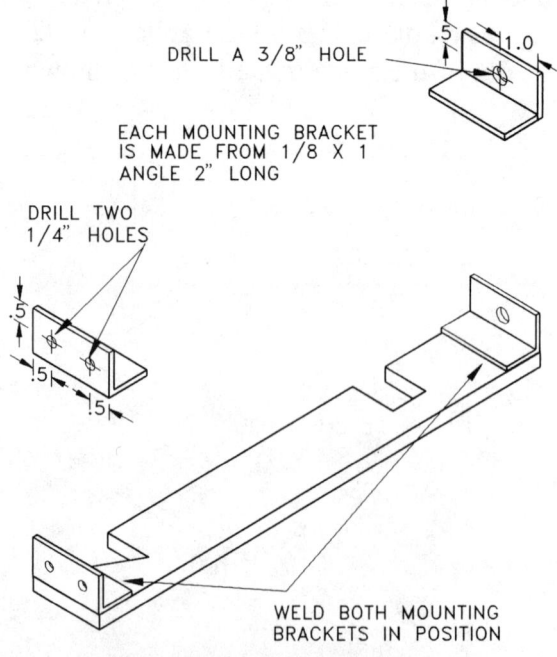

**Figure 73**  **Making the mounting brackets for the bottom cross brace and welding them in position.**

in the location shown. The blade wheel adjustment arm will mount here.

Drill four 1/4-20 holes in the side of the frame rail. Also drill and tap two additional holes 1/4-20.

The tapped holes are for mounting the upper blade wheel bearing assembly.

The rails for the upper blade guide rollers are mounted using the two drilled holes to the left of the tapped holes.

The drilled hole on each end is for mounting the rail to the front and rear post.

The left side top frame rail is also made from a piece of 1/4 x 1-1/2 angle 14" long. See fig. 75 for hole locations.

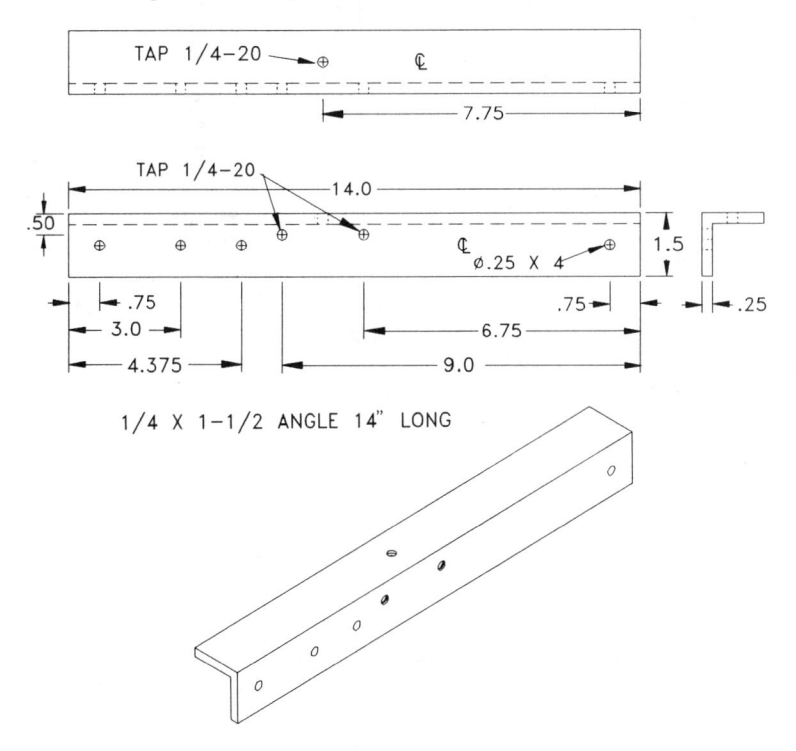

**Figure 74**     **The right side upper frame rail**

Drill and tap a 5/8-16 hole in the top of the frame rail at the location shown. This hole is for the blade wheel adjustment arm.

Drill a 1/4" hole on each end of the frame rail. These two holes are for mounting the frame rail to the front and rear post.

Make the front post from a piece of 3" channel 13" long. See fig. 76 for the hole locations.

Drill five 1/4" holes in the right side of the post as shown. These holes are for mounting the upper and lower frame rails and for mounting the blade guide back plate.

Drill four 1/4" holes in the front of the post. The two lower

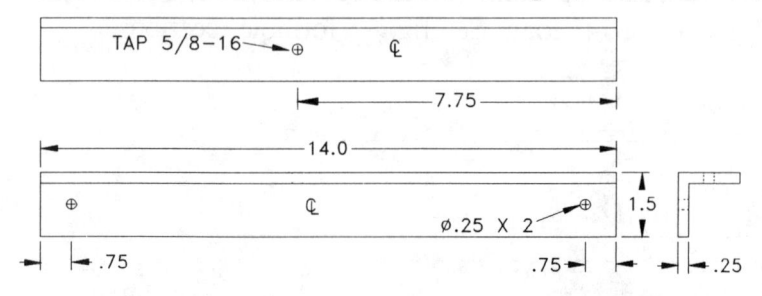

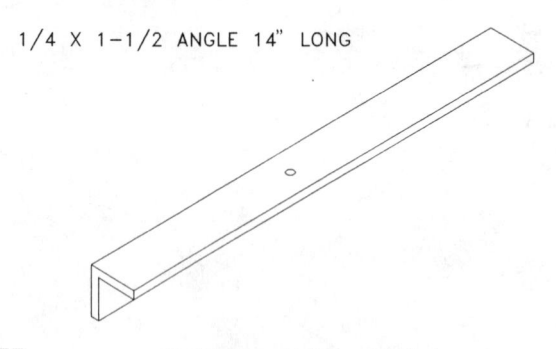

**Figure 75**     Left side top frame rail

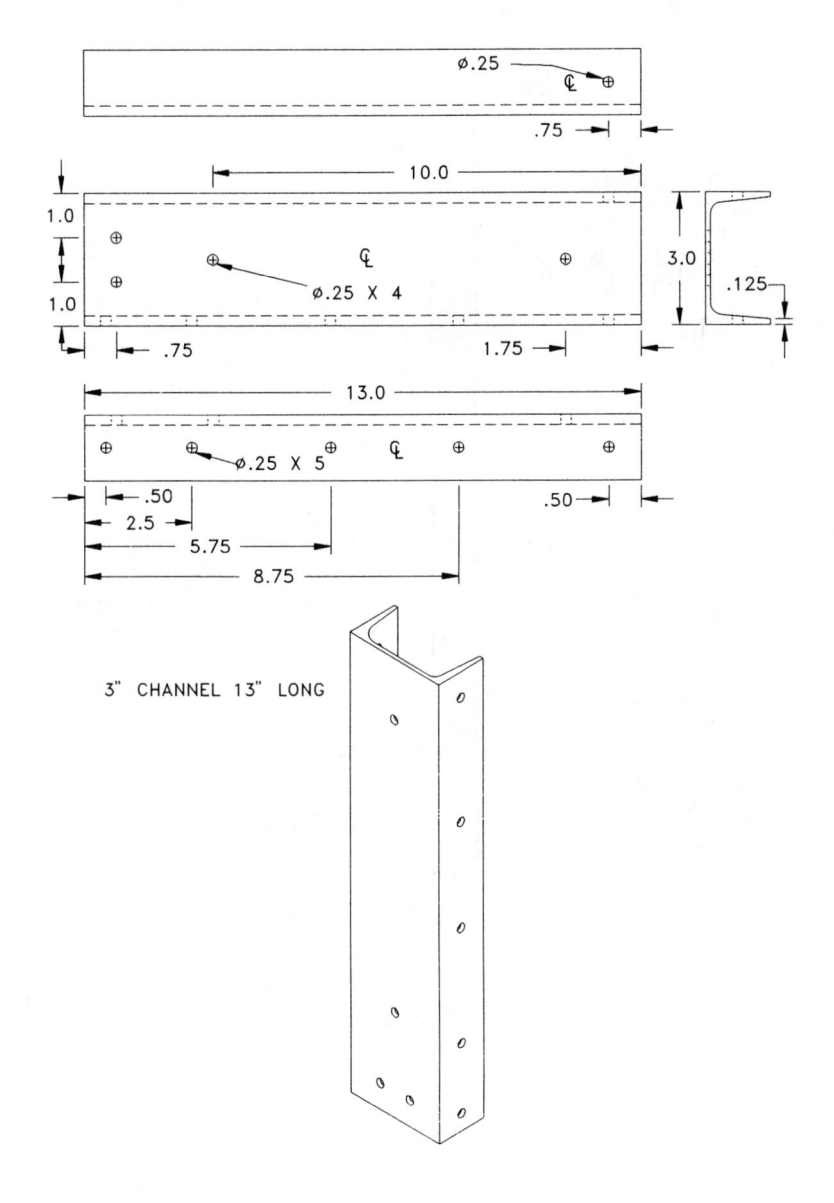

3" CHANNEL 13" LONG

**Figure 76**  Front post

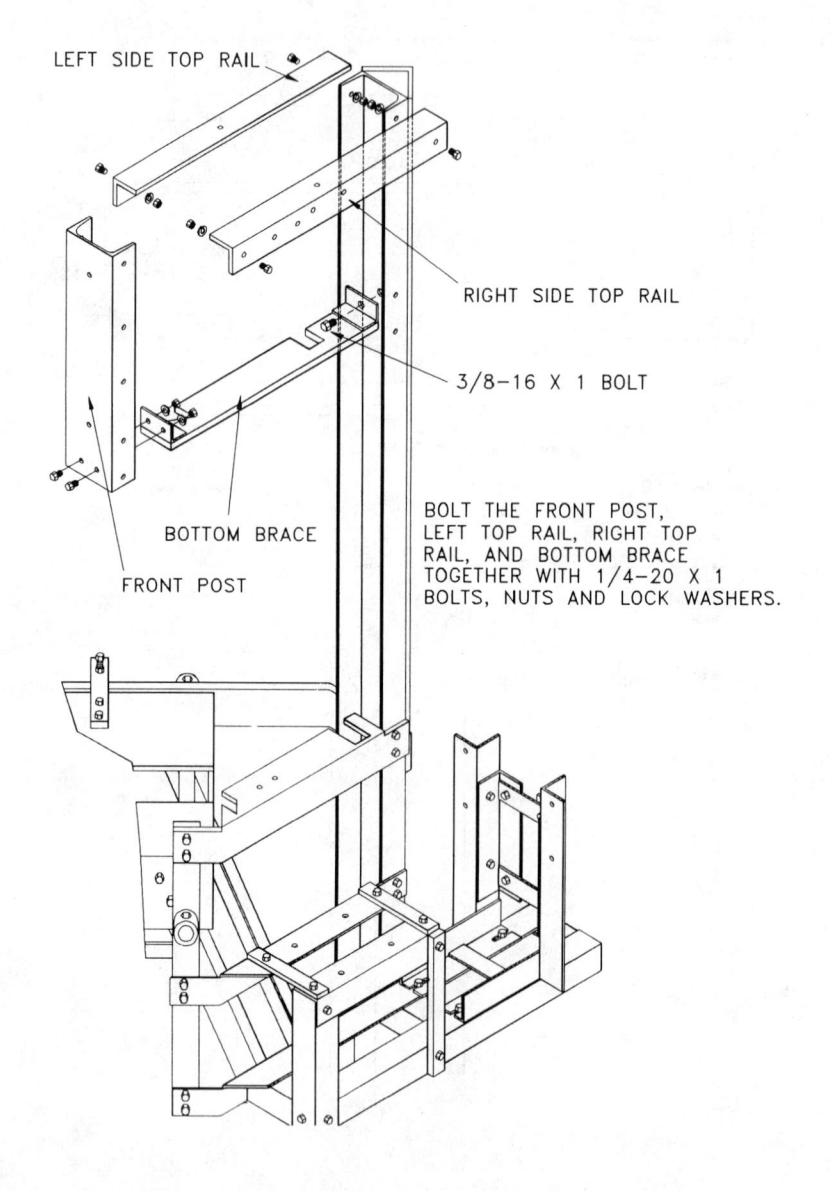

**Figure 77**   Assembling the upper vertical box frame

holes are for mounting the inside cross brace. The other two holes are for mounting the handle. Drill a 1/4" hole in the left side of the post. The left side frame rail mounts here.

Assemble the upper vertical box frame as shown in fig. 77. The bottom brace bolts to the rear vertical post with a 3/8-16 x 1 bolt, and to the front post with two 1/4-20 x 1 bolts, nuts and lock washers.

The right and left upper frame rails bolt to the front and rear post with 1/4-20 x 1 bolts, nuts and lock washers.

Make the right side bottom frame rail from a piece of 1/4 x 3 flat bar 14" long. For hole locations see fig. 78.

Drill two 1/4" holes in each end at the locations shown.

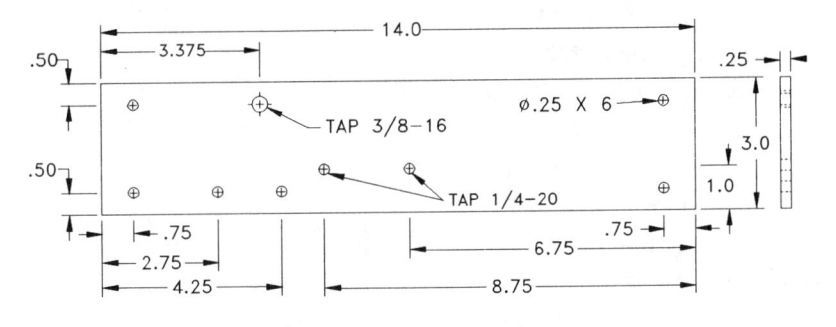

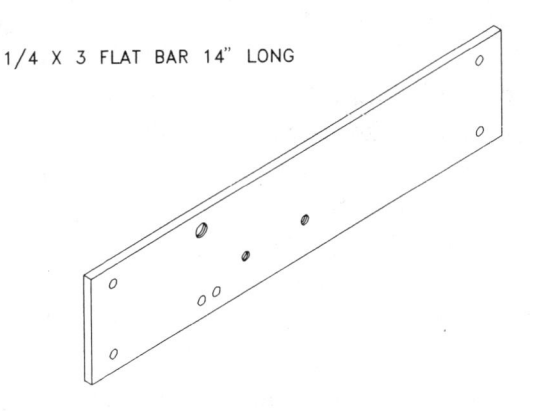

**Figure 78**     **Right side bottom frame rail**

These holes are for mounting the rail to the front and rear vertical post.

Drill and tap the 3/8-16 hole in the location shown if fig. 78. This hole is for mounting the adjustable blade guide assembly.

Drill the two 1/4" holes below it. These are for mounting the rails for the blade guide assembly.

Drill the other two 1/4" holes. These are for mounting the upper blade wheel bearing assembly.

Make the back plate for the blade guide assembly from a piece of 1/4 x 4 flat bar 5" long.

Drill two 1/4 " mounting holes in the locations shown in fig. 79.

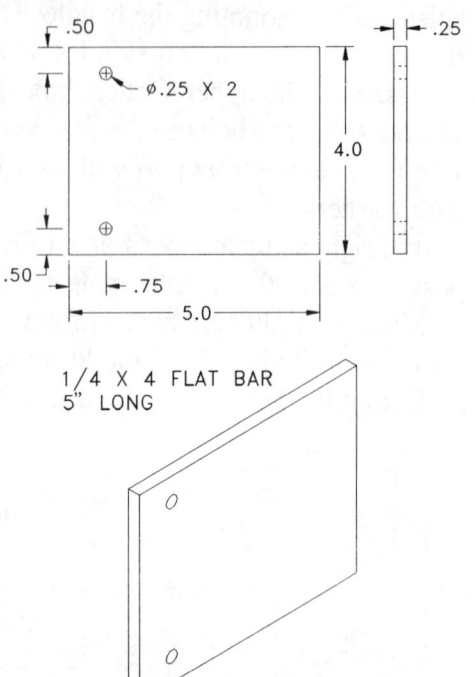

**Figure 79** Back plate for the upper blade guide assembly.

Bolt the back plate to the front post with 1/4-20 x 1 bolts, nuts and lock washers as shown in fig. 80.

Bolt the lower right side frame rail to the front and rear posts with 1/4-20 x 1 bolts, nuts and lock washers.

The adjustable upper blade guide assembly consists of a frame that adjusts up and down on a track.

Make the track from two pieces of 1/4 x 3/4 flat bar 13" long.

Drill a 1/4" hole in each end of each track as shown in figure 81. These holes are used to mount the track to the upper and

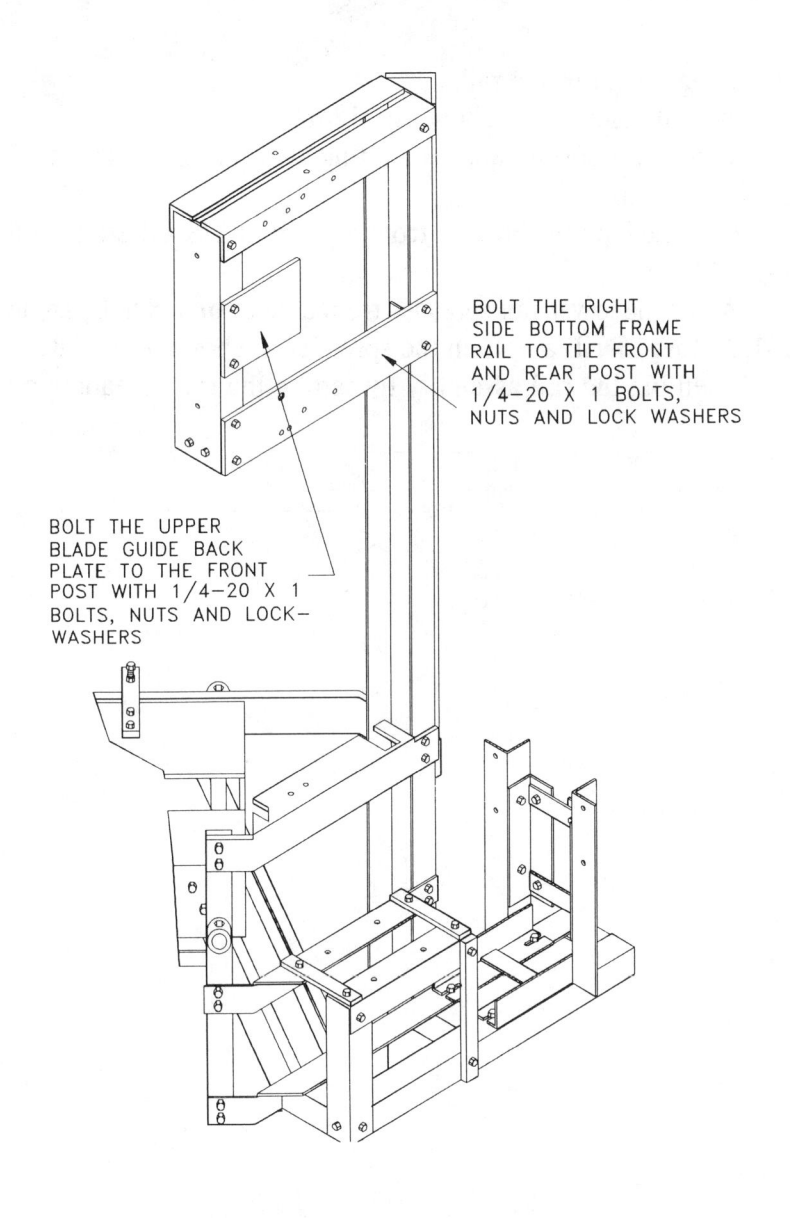

**Figure 80** Bolting the lower right side frame rail and the back plate for the blade guide assembly to the front and rear post.

lower right side frame rails.

The rail assembly is shown in fig. 82.

Make the outside rails by cutting two pieces of 1/8 x 1" angle 14" long.

Make the top rail spreader from a piece of 1/8 x 1 strap iron 2-1/2" long.

Make the lower rail spreader from a piece of 1/8 x 1" angle 2-1/2" long. Drill a hole in the spreader as shown in fig. 82.

Assemble the rail assembly by setting the rail spreaders on

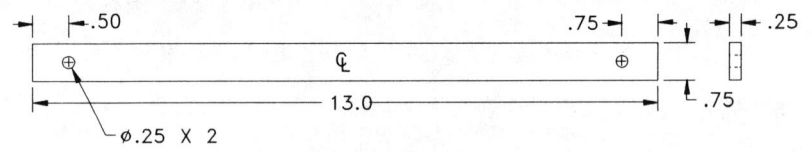

1/4 X 3/4 FLAT BAR 13" LONG

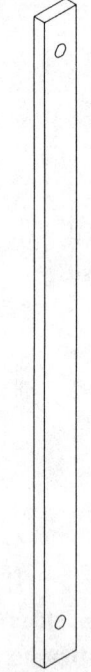

**Figure 81**     Track for the blade guide assembly. Make two.

|←——————14.0——————→| ┌1.0

RAILS FOR UPPER BLADE ROLLER ASSEMBLY
1/8 X 1 X 14 ANGLE
MAKE TWO

BOTTOM RAIL SPREADER
1/8 X 1 X 2-1/2 ANGLE
MAKE 1

TOP RAIL SPREADER
1/8 X 1 X 2-1/2 STRAP
MAKE 1

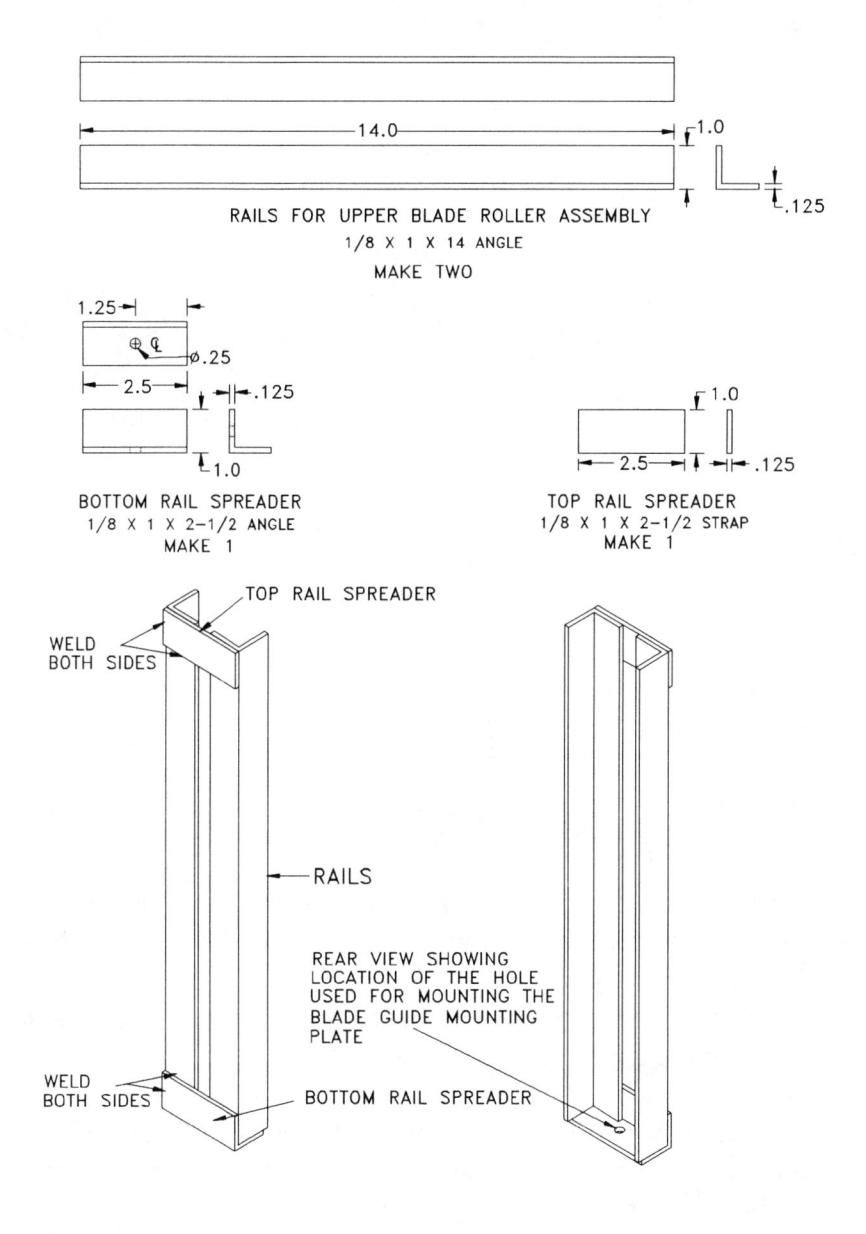

**Figure 82**     **Making the rail assembly**

3/8 SPACER BUSHING
7/8" LONG

3/8" FLAT WASHER

BOLT THE TRACK FOR THE RAIL ASSEMBLY TO THE UPPER AND LOWER SIDE RAILS WITH 1/4-20 X 1 BOLT, NUTS AND LOCK-WASHERS.

BOLT THE RAIL ASSEMBLY TO THE FRAME RAIL WITH A 3/8-16 X 2 BOLT

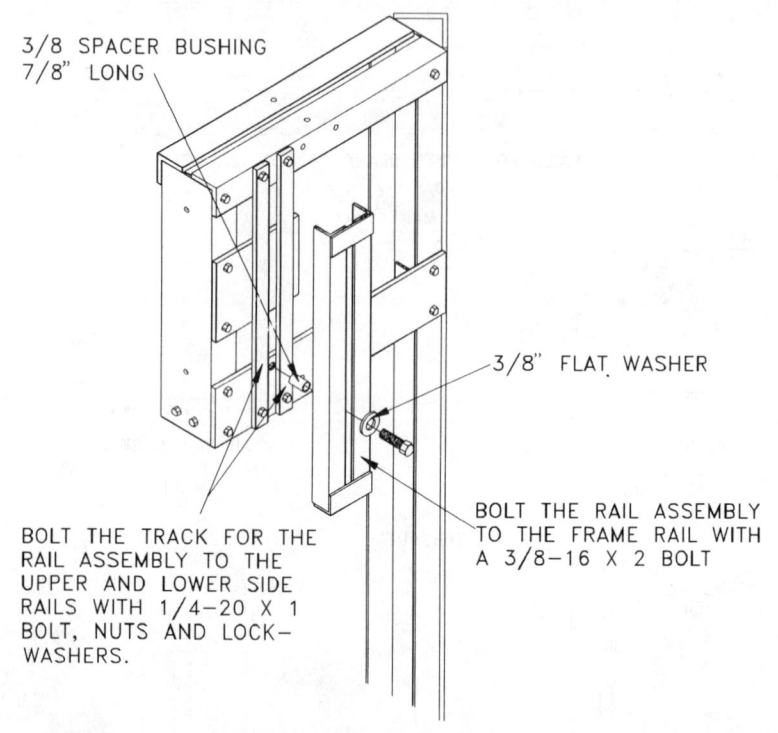

**Figure 83**   Bolting the blade guide and track to the upper vertical frame.

each end of the rails. Line up the rails so that the ends are even with the spreaders. Clamp in position and weld the spreaders to the rails. See fig. 82.

Bolt the rail assembly to the upper and lower right side frame rails on the upper vertical frame as shown in fig. 83. Use 1/4-20 x 1 bolts, nuts and lock washers. The rail assembly is held in position with a 3/8-16 x 2 bolt. A flat washer is used with the bolt to keep the head of the bolt from going between the rails.

A 3/8" bushing 7/8" long is used between the rail assembly

and the frame rail. This gives the bolt something to tighten against and prevents the frame from warping as it is tightened.

The rail assembly raises and lowers the blade guide rollers. When they are in the desired position the bolt is tightened and the frame is held firmly in position.

## BUILDING THE IDLER WHEEL MOUNTING ASSEMBLY

The idler wheel mounting assembly not only supports the wheel shaft, it also adjusts the blade tension and the tilt angle of the idler wheel. We can break the mounting assembly into three sub assemblies. They are the bearing assembly, the frame assembly and the tension adjustment assembly.

**THE IDLER WHEEL BEARING ASSEMBLY:** First you need two bearings with a 3/4" hub. The bearings used are an inexpensive general purpose type. Most of the hardware stores I have visited have these bearings. They are usually found in the same area as the bronze bushings or in the lawn mower parts department. This type of bearing is often used for small utility wheels, such as those used on lawn mowers, wheel barrows, dollies, etc.

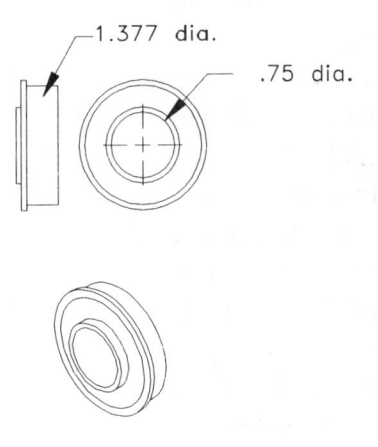

**Figure 84** The idler wheel bearing

Fig. 84 shows a drawing of the bearing. Notice that the hub has a lip that sticks out on one side about 1/16" past the main body. The purpose of this lip will become more evident later on.

The main body of the bearing also has a lip to prevent the bearing from being pressed too far into the housing.

The bearings are placed in each end of a 3-1/2" length of 1-1/4" black pipe. The pipe is referred to as the bearing housing. A drawing of the bearing housing is shown in fig. 85.

One end of the pipe is threaded 1-1/4-12. There is no need to buy an expensive die to cut the threads. Short sections of pipe that are already threaded can be bought cheaply at most hardware stores.

The inside diameter of 1-1/4 black pipe varies. The spec. size is supposed to be around 1.380. Since the outside diameter of our bearing measures approximately 1.377 this would be ideal. If you are lucky enough to obtain a piece of 1-1/4 pipe that measures 1.380 I.D. just clean up the burr edge and press a bearing in each end. If the pipe is too large, you will need to shim the bearings. I had to shim mine .010. If the pipe

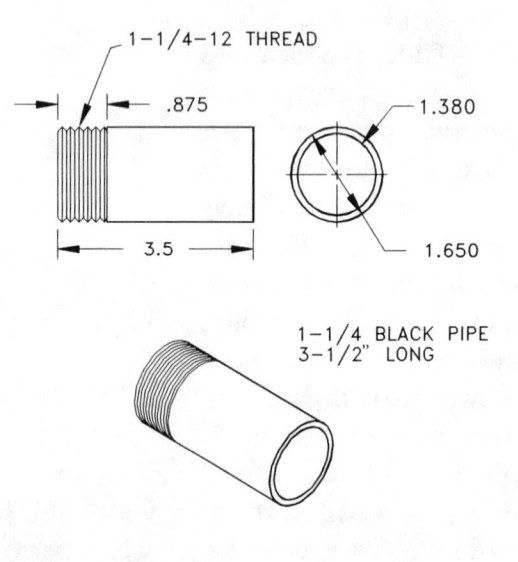

**Figure 85** Idler wheel bearing housing

7.0

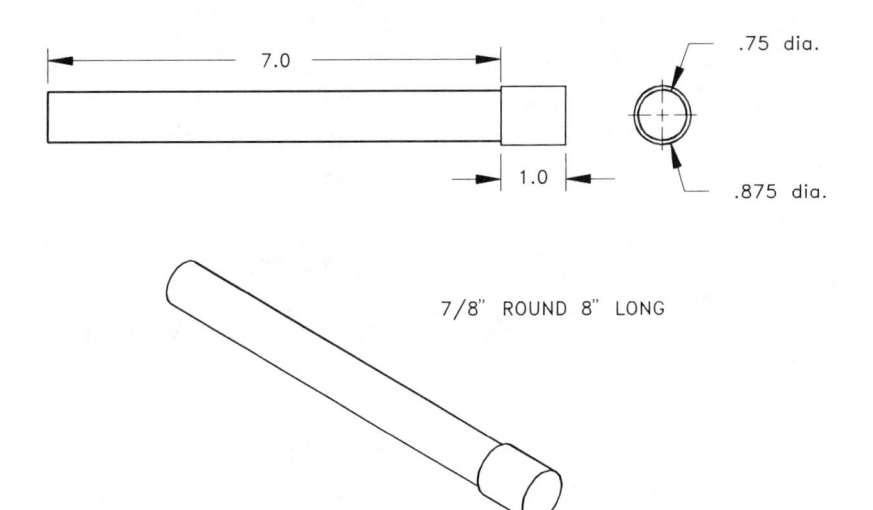

1.0

.75 dia.

.875 dia.

7/8" ROUND 8" LONG

**Figure 86**     The idler wheel shaft

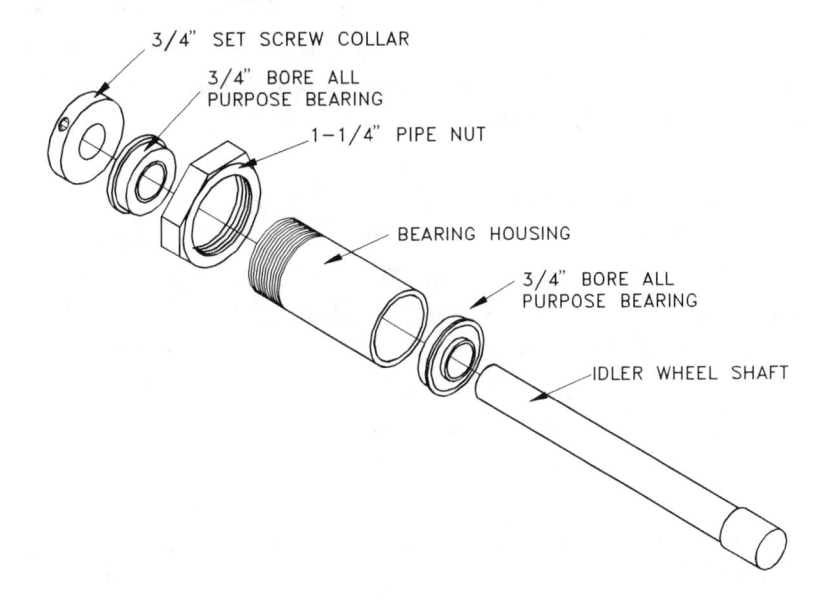

3/4" SET SCREW COLLAR
3/4" BORE ALL PURPOSE BEARING
1-1/4" PIPE NUT
BEARING HOUSING
3/4" BORE ALL PURPOSE BEARING
IDLER WHEEL SHAFT

**Figure 87**     The idler wheel bearing assembly

is to small you will need to bore it out larger.

The idler wheel shaft is made from a piece of 7/8" round rod 10" long. The finished length of the shaft will be 8". I allowed the extra material length to give the lathe chuck a firm grip.

Mount one end of the shaft in a three jaw chuck and turn a 7" length of the shaft to a .75 diam. See fig. 86.

The length of the 7/8" diam. end of the shaft need only be 1" long, so cut the 2" excess off.

Look at fig. 87 as we begin putting the idler wheel bearing assembly together.

Screw a 1-1/4" pipe nut on the threaded end of the bearing housing, then press a bearing in each end of the housing.

Insert the idler wheel shaft through the bearings until the edge of 7/8" diameter end is flush against the lip of the bearing hub.

Slide a 3/4" set screw collar over the other end of the shaft. push it tightly against the lip of the other bearing hub and tighten the set screw. In operation the bearing hub is held stationary while the outer ring turns.

**THE IDLER WHEEL FRAME ASSEMBLY:** The frame assembly is constructed entirely of 1/2 x 1/2 bar stock. Its individual parts are shown in fig. 88. The purpose of the frame is to hold the bearing assembly in place, but still allow it to move in a track, up and down to adjust blade tension. The frame can also be adjusted to control the tilt of the idler wheel.

The main parts of the frame are the inside frame rails, the spacer bars and the outer rails.

Make each of the two inside frame rails from a piece of 1/2 x 1/2 bar stock 13" long. Drill three 1/4" holes in the locations shown. Drill and tap the fourth hole 1/4-20. The tapped holes are for the tilt adjustment bolts.

Make a 1/4" deep cut in the frame the width of a saw blade at the location shown in fig. 88. The purpose of the cut is to weaken the frame creating a pivot point for the tilt adjustment

INSIDE FRAME RAIL FOR UPPER
BLADE WHEEL BEARING ASSEMBLY.

MAKE TWO

SPACER
MAKE TWO

ALL PIECES MADE FROM
1/2 X 1/2 BAR STOCK

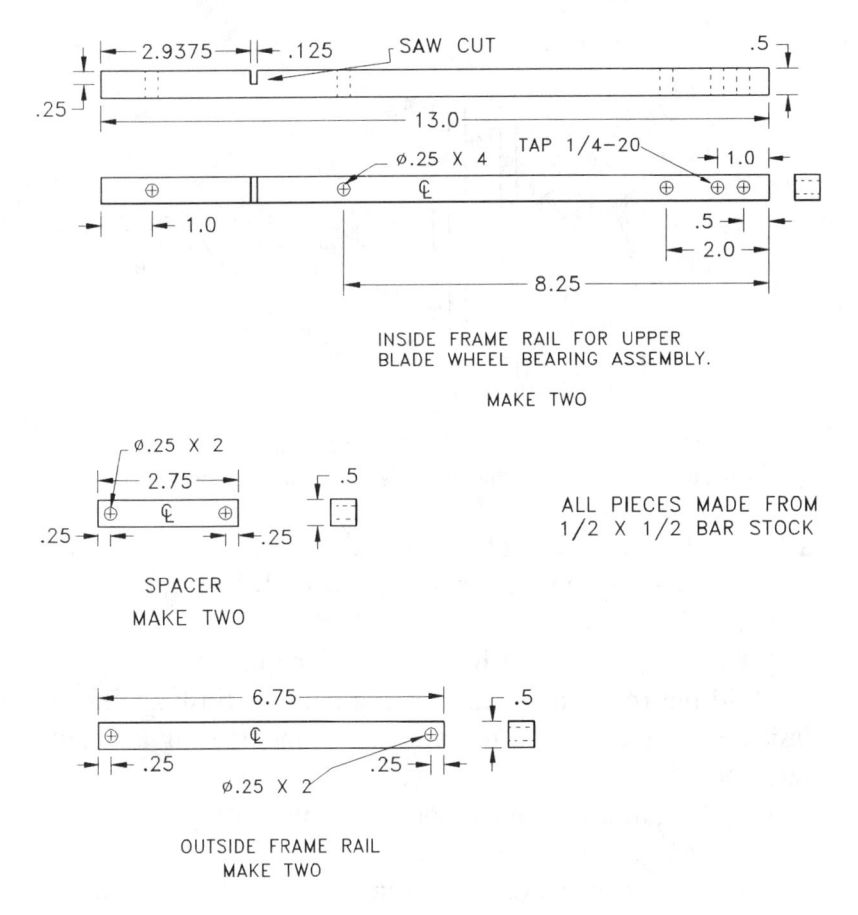

OUTSIDE FRAME RAIL
MAKE TWO

**Figure 88**  **Parts for the idler wheel frame assembly**

of the idler wheel. As the tilt adjustment bolts are tightened, the frame bends at the cut point and causes the idler wheel to tilt back. This adjustment is necessary to adjust the way the saw blade tracks on the wheel.

Make the two spacer bars from 1/2 x 1/2 bar stock and drill

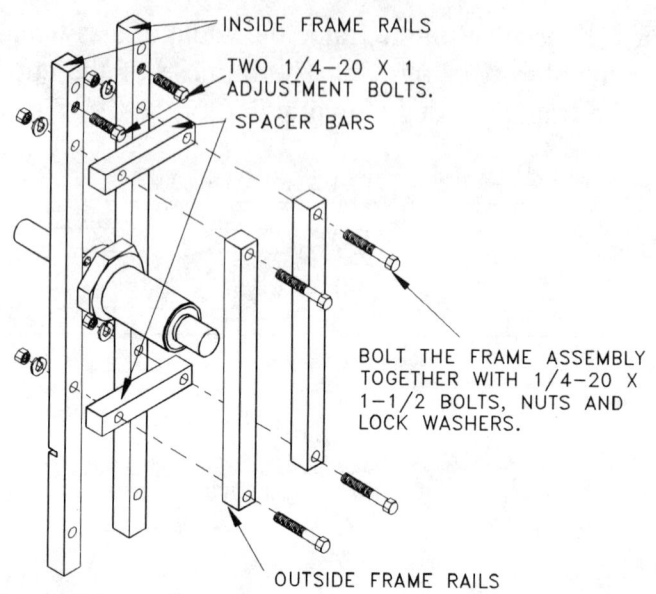

**Figure 89**   Bolting the idler wheel frame assembly together

a 1/4" hole at each end of both bars.

The two outside rails are also made from 1/2 x 1/2 bar stock. Drill a 1/4" hole in each end of both rails.

Refer to fig. 89 as we begin assembling the frame.

Hold the front end of the bearing housing flush against the inside rail of the frame. The front end of the housing is the end with the pipe nut.

Bolt the spacer bars and outer rails in position with 1/4-20 x 1-1/2 bolts, nuts and lock washers.

The 1-1/4" pipe nut on the bearing housing should fit in such a way that it slides freely up and down in the frame assembly. If it has too much play it will affect the tilt range of the idler wheel. If it is too tight it will bind.

If necessary, you can widen the track with shims. The track can be narrowed by grinding a little bit off of the front side of the outer rails in the area where they bolt to the spacer bars.

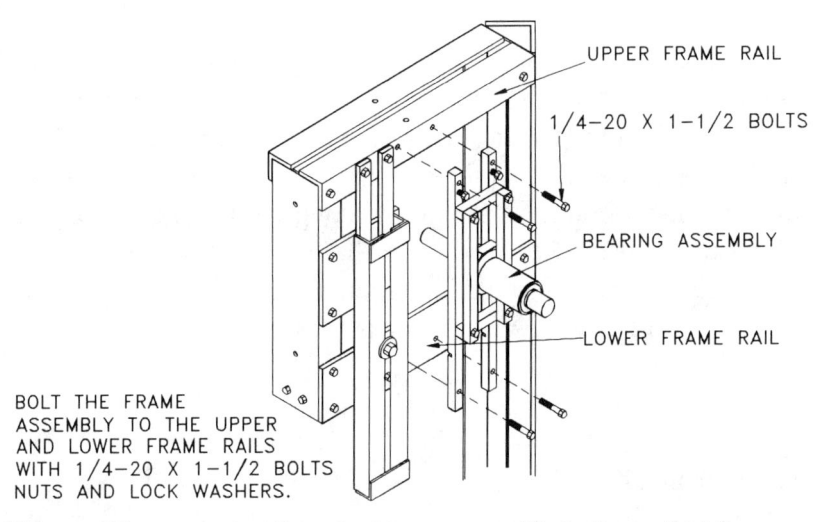

**Figure 90** Bolting the idler wheel frame assembly to the vertical frame

Screw a 1/4-20 x 1 adjustment bolt into the threaded hole located in each inside frame rail. Bolt the idler wheel assembly to the upper and lower frame rails located on the upper vertical saw frame. Use 1/4-20 x 1-1/2 bolts. See Fig. 90.

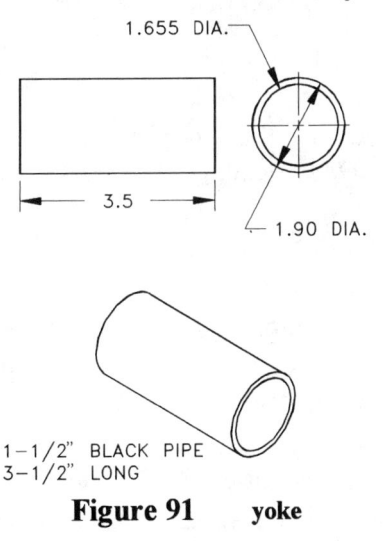

**THE BLADE TENSION ADJUSTMENT ASSEMBLY:** To briefly describe the assembly, the yoke which is a 3-1/2" long piece of 1-1/2" black pipe, slides over the idler wheel bearing housing. It has a 1/2-13 x 1-3/4 coupling nut welded on the outside of it.

**Figure 91**  yoke

109

The stationary arm is bolted to the top of the vertical frame. It extends out, over and directly above the idler wheel bearing assembly.

The adjustment bolt is a 1/2-13 x 8 bolt that fits in the slot at the end of the stationary arm. A set screw collar is mounted on the bolt and placed flush against the underside of the stationary arm and holds the bolt in position. The other end of the adjustment bolt threads into the coupling nut that is welded to the top of the yoke.

As the adjustment bolt is tightened the idler wheel raises, tightening the blade. As the bolt is loosened, the wheel drops and loosens the blade.

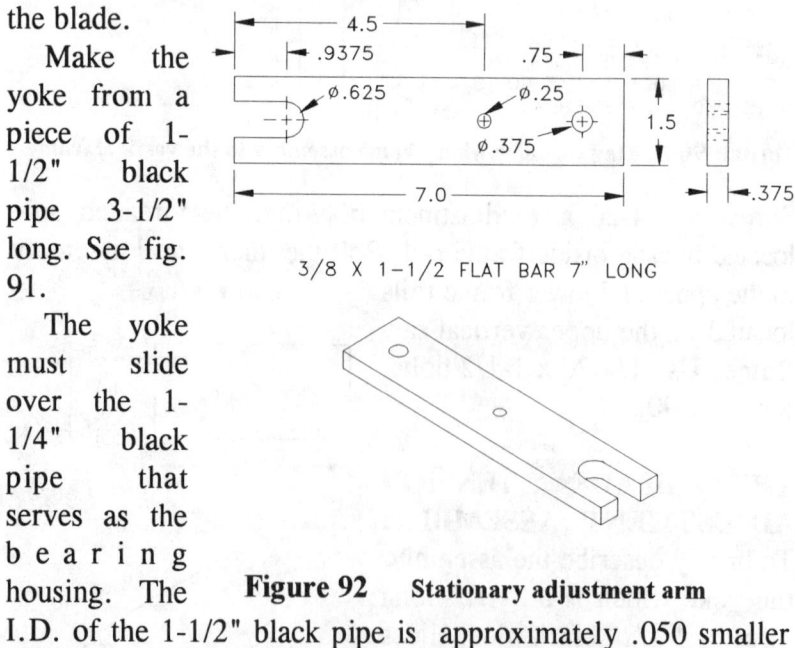

Make the yoke from a piece of 1-1/2" black pipe 3-1/2" long. See fig. 91.

The yoke must slide over the 1-1/4" black pipe that serves as the bearing housing. The I.D. of the 1-1/2" black pipe is approximately .050 smaller than the O.D. of the 1-1/4 black pipe, so you will have increase the I.D. of the pipe approximately .050.

Mount the 1-1/2" pipe in a 3 jaw chuck and bore it to a size sufficient to allow it to slide over the 1-1/4" black pipe.

**Figure 92**  Stationary adjustment arm

3/8 X 1-1/2 FLAT BAR 7" LONG

The stationary adjustment arm is shown in figure 92.
Make it from a piece of 3/8 x 1-1/2 flat bar 7" long.
Drill a 3/8" hole and a 1/4" hole in the locations shown.
Cut a 5/8" wide slot in one end of the arm. The slot is for the adjustment bolt.

Refer to fig. 93 as we begin mounting the adjustment assembly.

Bolt the stationary arm to the top of the vertical frame with a 3/8-16 x 1 bolt and a 1/4-20 x 1 bolt.

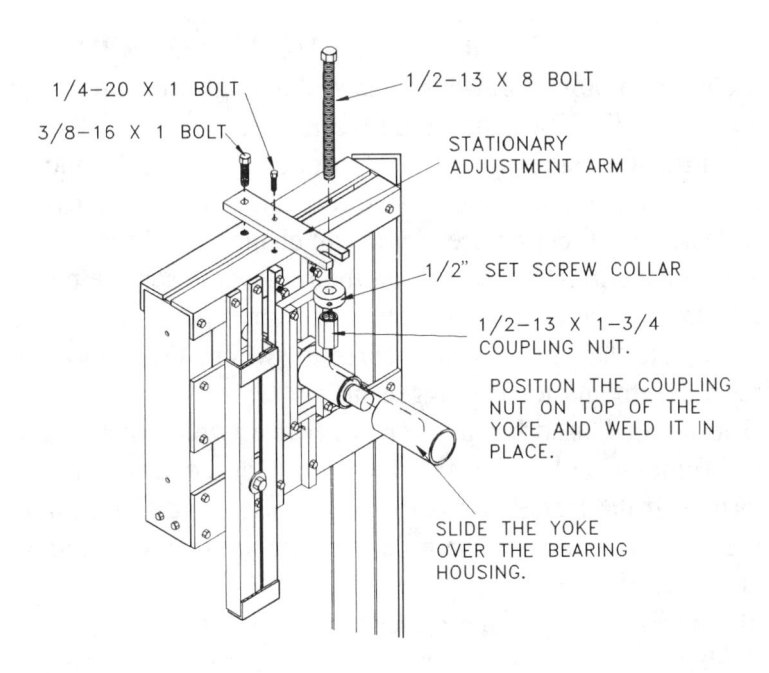

**Figure 93**   Mounting the blade tension adjustment assembly

111

Slide the yoke over the bearing housing so that it is flush against the frame.

Slip a 1/2" set screw collar over the end of the 1/2-13 x 8" adjustment bolt. Also thread the 1/2 x 13 x 1-3/4 coupling nut on the end of the bolt. Slide the adjustment bolt into the slot in the stationary adjustment arm.

Adjust the bolt so that it is straight and the coupling nut is in position at the top of the yoke. When the coupling nut is in position, weld or braze it to the top of the yoke.

## THE BELT DRIVE ASSEMBLY

**CHOOSING A MOTOR:** I used a 1/2 HP, 1750 RPM, 120 volt electric motor to power my saw. Although I haven't tried it, I think a 1/3 HP motor would work fine.

To turn the blade wheel in the proper direction the motor must turn in a counter clockwise direction. If your motor runs in a clock wise direction see if you can change the direction by reversing the wires located behind the removable service plate. Many times there is a small wiring diagram on the back of the service plate that shows which wires to switch. Do not switch wires while the motor is plugged in.

The motor I used has a Nema 48 frame, which means that the mounting holes are 3" between slot centers and 5" vertically. If the frame on the motor you use has different hole locations simply change the hole locations in the motor mount rails in fig. 65.

If the RPM rating of the motor you want to use is different, the pulley sizes will have to be changed. If that is the case see the next section, "Deciding which pulleys to use".

**DECIDING WHICH PULLEYS TO USE:** I will describe the methods I used to decide which pulleys to use. If you are using a motor with a different RPM rating or if you want the saw blade to travel at a faster or slower speed you can use the followings formulas to arrive at pulley sizes.

In our configuration, a 1-1/2" A-size pulley is on the motor shaft. The motor pulley is connected by a 30" "V" belt to the 8" A-size out board pulley on the counter shaft. A 1-3/4" A-size pulley is located on the center of the counter shaft and it is connected by a 30" "V" belt to a 6" A-size pulley on the drive shaft.

One of the first things to remember is that A-size pulleys have a pitch diameter that is 1/4" less than their outside diameter.

To determine the speed of the counter shaft, divide the pitch diameter of the larger outboard pulley on the counter shaft by the pitch diameter of the smaller motor pulley. (7.75÷1.25=6.2) which is our reduction ratio (6.2-1). Divide the speed of the motor by the reduction ratio. (1750÷6.2=282.26). This tells us that the counter shaft is turning at 282.26 RPM.

To determine the speed of the drive shaft, divide the pitch diameter of the larger drive shaft pulley by the pitch diameter of the smaller counter shaft pulley. (5.75÷1.5=3.83). Divide the speed of the counter shaft by the reduction ratio. (282.26÷3.83=73.7). This tells us that the drive shaft is turning at 73.7 RPM.

Blade speed on a bandsaw is determined by the number of feet per minute that the blade is traveling. When figuring your desired blade speed, remember that the size of the blade wheels will have a definite effect on the speed. The larger the wheel the faster the blade, and the smaller the wheel the slower the blade.

To find the blade speed we must first determine the

circumference of the blade wheel. The formula for that is, $C = 3.146D$. The finished diameter of our blade wheel will be 8.25, so ($3.146 \times 8.25" = 25.95"$).

To find the blade speed in inches per minute multiply the speed of the drive shaft by the circumference of the blade wheel in inches. ($25.95" \times 73.7$ rpm $= 1912.5"$). To convert to feet per

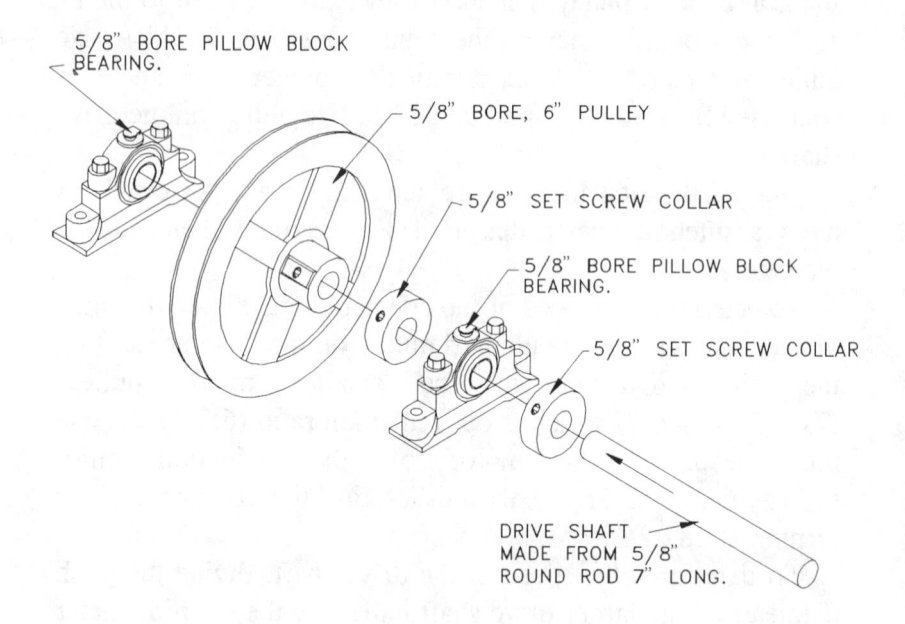

**Figure 94**      **The drive shaft**

minute divide the speed in inches by 12". ($1912.5" \div 12" = 159.37$ feet per minute), which is a good speed for cutting mild steel.

**THE DRIVE SHAFT AND COUNTERSHAFT:** The **drive shaft** layout is shown in fig. 94. Cut a 7" length of 5/8" round rod for the drive shaft. You will also need two 5/8" set screw collars, a 5/8" bore 6" A-size pulley, and two 5/8" bore, bronze sleeve pillow block bearings. Notice that the pillow block bearings used for the drive shaft are solid mount. I used bronze sleeve bearings because they are much cheaper than ball bearing. No doubt, ball bearings would be much better. I did some experimentation with the cheaper resilient type bearings often used on fan motors, and found that they did not provide enough stability for the drive shaft.

I bought the pillow block bearings from the local hardware store. They are available in either bronze sleeved or ball bearing in sizes up to 3/4". The pillow block bearings I used for the drive shaft in this project are manufactured by Chicago Die Cast, 9148 King Street, Franklin Park, IL 60131. The model

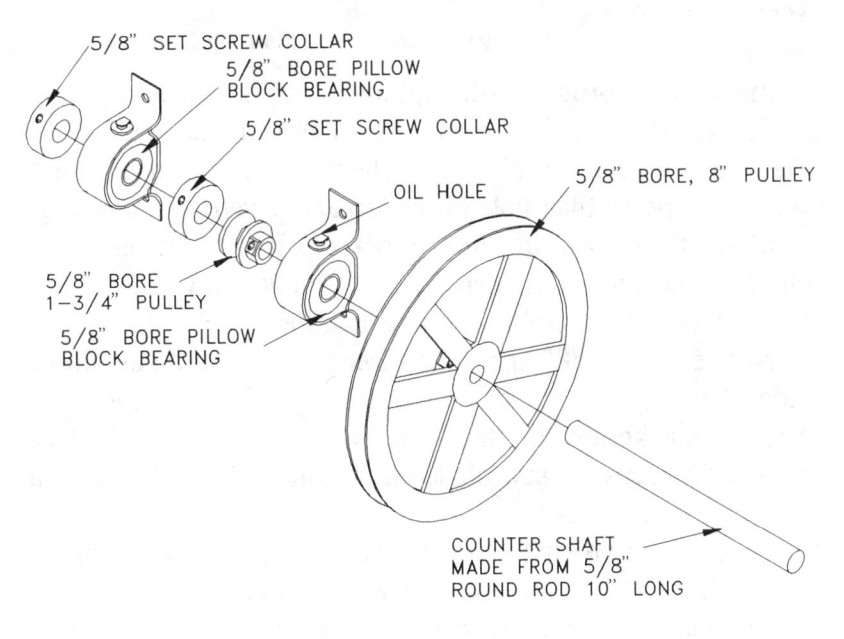

**Figure 95**      **The counter shaft**

number is 7-500-6, 5/8.

**The counter shaft** layout is shown in fig. 95. Cut a 10" length of 5/8" round rod for the shaft. You will also need a 5/8" bore 8" A-size pulley, a 1-3/4" A-size pulley, two 5/8" set screw collars and two resilient mount bronze bushed pillow block bearings.

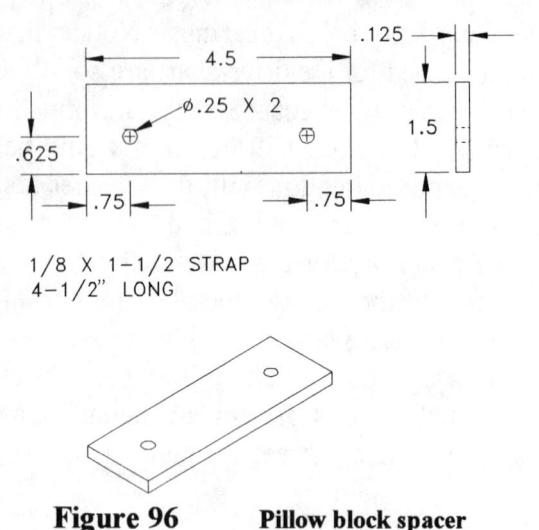

**Figure 96**    Pillow block spacer

The cheaper resilient mount bearings work just fine here. They need to be universal mount. The universal mount type lets you locate the oil filler hole for horizontal or vertical mounting.

Mount the drive shaft pillow block bearings to the inner and outer frame rails on the drive shaft stand as shown in fig. 97. Use 1/4-20 x 1-1/2 bolts with nuts and lock washers.

Notice that a 1/8" spacer is placed under the outer pillow block bearing. The spacer raises the back of the drive shaft causing the bottom of the blade wheel to tilt inward. This inward tilt keeps the saw blade on the wheel. See fig. 96 for a drawing of the spacer.

Slide the drive shaft into the pillow block bearings along with a 30" "V" belt, two set screw collars and a 5/8" bore 6" A-size pulley. Refer back to fig. 94 for the drive shaft configuration.

Place the set screw collars flush against each side of the outside pillow block. The outside end of the drive shaft will be flush with the outer edge of the outside set screw collar. Tighten the set screws.

Center the 6" pulley in the center opening of the drive shaft stand and tighten the set screw.

Loosen the set screws and remove the drive shaft. You should be able to see the marks in the shaft made by the set

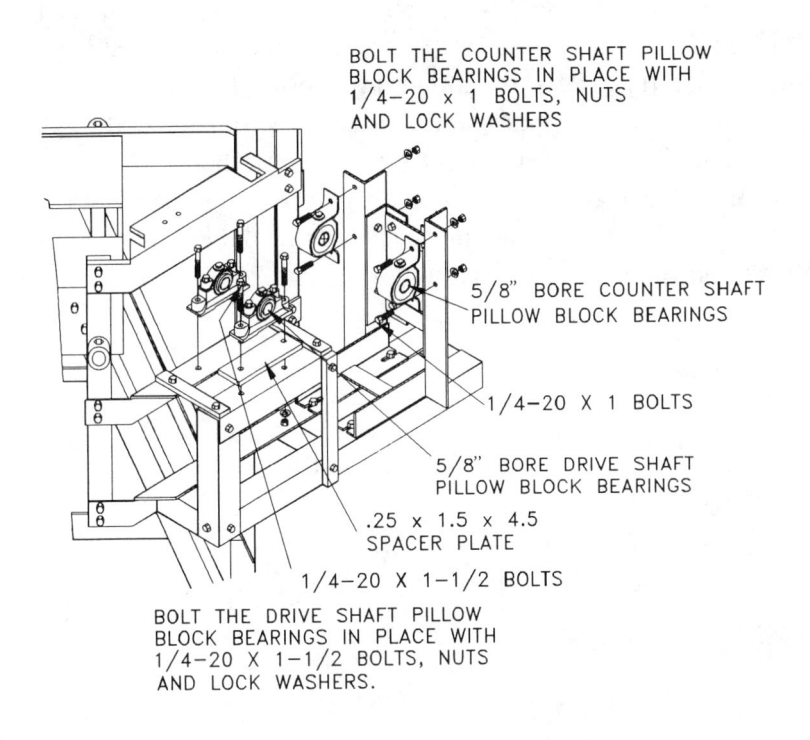

**Figure 97**   Bolting the pillow block bearings in place

screws. At each mark, grind or file a flat spot on the shaft. The flat spots will give the set screws a solid seat and will prevent the pulley from slipping on the shaft during operation of the saw. After the flat spots are ground replace the shaft and retighten all set screws making sure they seat on the flat spots.

Unbolt one side of the rear cross brace on the drive shaft

stand. Slide it to one side and pull the "V" belt through. Slide the brace back in position and bolt it in place. See fig. 99.

Bolt the counter shaft pillow block bearings to the counter shaft stand with 1/4-20 x 1 bolts, nuts and lock washers.

Slide the counter shaft through the pillow block bearings along with the other end of the 30" "V" belt, the 5/8" bore, 1-3/4" pulley, the two set screw collars and the 8" outboard pulley. See fig. 95 for the mounting configuration.

Mount the 8" outboard pulley flush on the outside end of the counter shaft and tighten the set screw. Align the 1-3/4" pulley with the 6" drive shaft pulley and tighten the set screw. Place a set screw collar flush against each side of the left side pillow block and tighten the set screws.

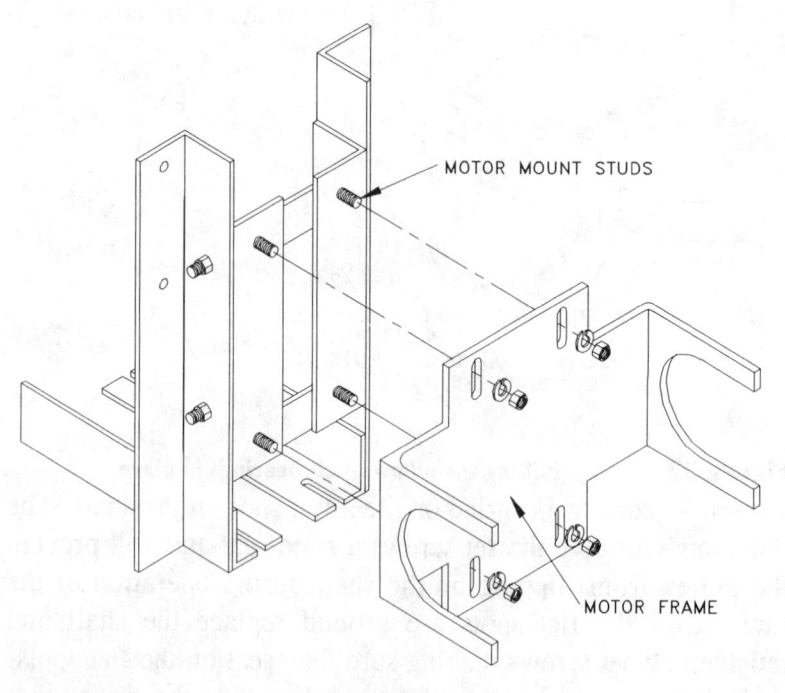

**Figure 98**     **Mounting the motor**

Loosen the set screws, remove the counter shaft and grind the flat spots on the counter shaft. Replace the shaft and retighten the set screws making sure they seat on the flat spots. Slip the "V" belt over the 6" drive shaft pulley and the 1-3/4" counter shaft pulley. Adjust the belt tension by moving the counter shaft stand back. Tighten the counter shaft stand bolts.

**MOUNTING THE MOTOR:** Bolt the motor to the motor mount. Fig 98 shows a rear view of the counter shaft stand and motor mount. The motor frame is shown without the motor for clarity. The slots in the motor frame allow us to move the motor

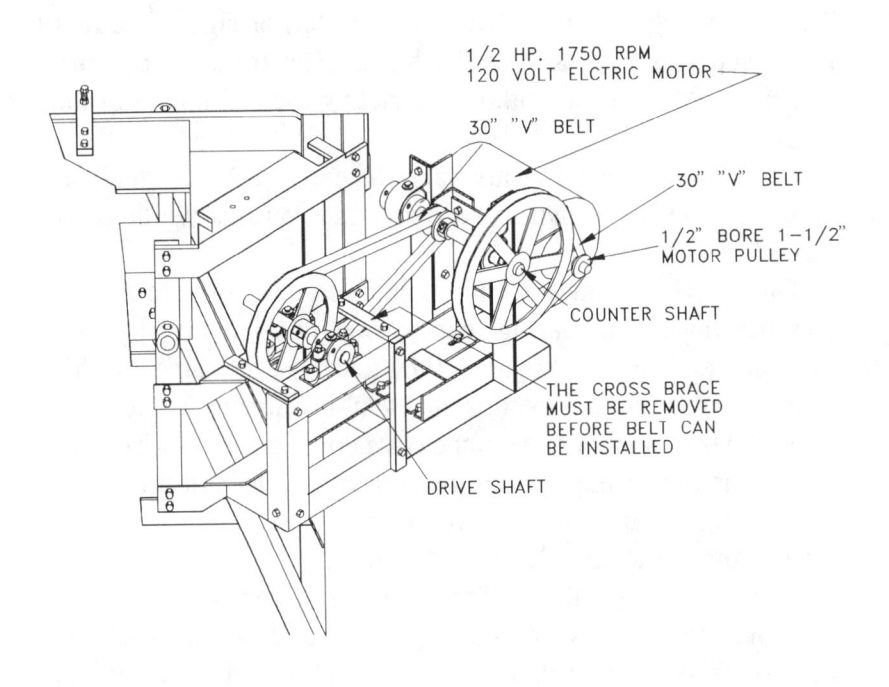

**Figure 99**     The drive assembly complete

up and down to adjust the belt tension.

Place a 1-1/2" pulley on the end of the motor shaft. Tighten the set screw.

Slip a 30" "V" belt over the 8" out board pulley and the 1-1/2" motor pulley. Adjust the belt tension and tighten the motor mount nuts.

## THE BLADE GUIDES

There are two sets of blade guides, the upper and lower. Each blade guide assembly consists of three rollers. Two side rollers are used to hold the blade in a straight vertical position. They also keep the blade from twisting left or right. The rear roller supports the back of the blade. The rollers must turn freely and do their job without restricting the movement of the blade.

The lower guide is stationary. The upper blade guide is adjustable up and down to accommodate various width work pieces.

On commercial saws, the blade guide rollers used are double row bearings. The bearings can be bought commercially, but they are expensive. About $10.00 each at the time of this printing. We need 6 of them, so the total investment would have been $60.00. In order to keep the costs down on our project we made our own using bronze bushings. The rollers are made from 1-1/2" diam. cold roll round rod. The eccentric bolt is made from a 1/2-13 x 2, grade 6 bolt.

The surface of the rollers and the eccentric bolt were hardened using "case hardening compound. I followed the directions on the back of the can and found that surface hardening is really a simple process. The instructions are as follows.

You will be working with high heat and an open flame so

remember to take the appropriate safety precautions.

1. Heat the part to a bright red(approximately 1650 degrees F.) 2.Dip or roll the part in the hardening compound to form a fused shell around the area to be hardened and then reheat the area to a bright red.

3. Quench the part immediately in clean, cold water using a scrubbing action to insure maximum cooling rate.

**MAKING THE ROLLERS:** The rollers are made from 1-1/2" diam. cold roll round rod. Each roller is bored .750 and is 3/8" wide.

You can make all 6 of them on the lathe at once by placing a 6" length of 1-1/2" diam. cold roll in a 3-jaw chuck. You only need about 3-1/2" of the material, but using a 6" length gives enough for the chuck to grip.

Generally the outside surface of cold roll is fairly uniform, but it is important to true it up on the lathe anyway.

Bore a hole in the

BLADE GUIDE ROLLER IS MADE FROM 1-1/2 DIA. COLD ROLL ROUND ROD 3/8" LONG

5/8 I.D. BRONZE BUSHING 7/16" LONG

INSERT THE BRONZE BUSHING INSIDE THE GUIDE ROLLER.

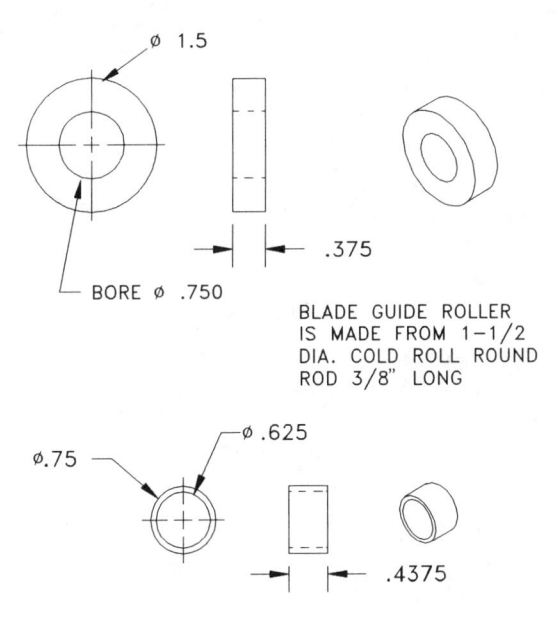

**Figure 100** Blade guide roller. Make 6

round rod to approximately .750, or until a 5/8" I.D. bushing will press fit in the hole. See fig. 100.

Cut six 3/8" wide rollers from the round stock. They can be cut with a lathe cut off tool or a hacksaw. Make sure that the cut is straight.

You will need six 5/8" I.D. x 3/4"O.D. bronze bushings 7/16" long. Press a bushing into each guide roller. The bushing will extend out 1/32" from each side of the guide roller.

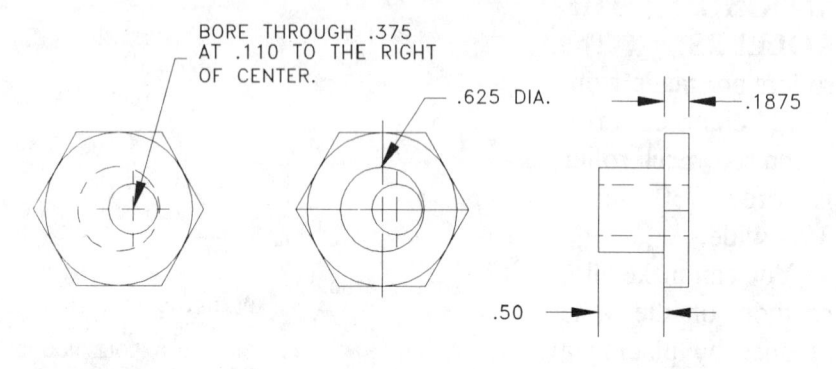

BORE THROUGH .375 AT .110 TO THE RIGHT OF CENTER.

.625 DIA.

.1875

.50

ECCENTRIC ADJUSTMENT BOLT IS MADE FROM A 3/4 X 1 GRADE SIX BOLT.

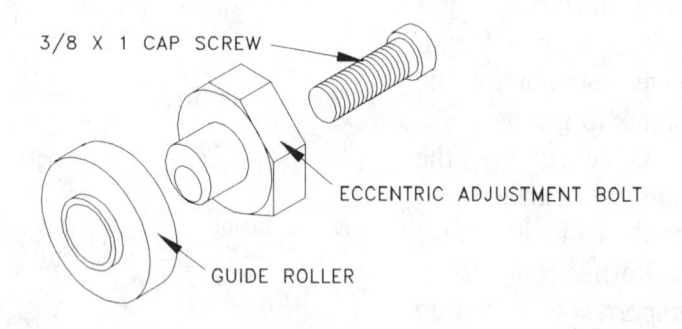

3/8 X 1 CAP SCREW

ECCENTRIC ADJUSTMENT BOLT

GUIDE ROLLER

**Figure 101**  **The eccentric bolt. Make 6**

**THE ECCENTRIC BOLT:** The purpose of the eccentric bolt is to give the guide rollers an adjustment range. By adjusting the rollers you can straighten the blade vertically and move it from left to right.

The eccentric bolts are made from 1/2-13 x 3 bolts and you will need 6 of them. Because the bolts will be case hardened you will need to use at least a grade 6. You can tell the grade by the number of slashes on the head of the bolt. Each slash represents two grade points, so a grade 6 will have 3 slashes.

Fig. 101 shows the specifications for the eccentric bolt. One way to turn the outside shaft of the bolt, is to place head of the bolt in a four jaw chuck and center it as close as possible. The outside of the bolt shaft is turned to approximately .625. File finish the bolt shaft until it fits nicely in the bushing located in the guide roller.

There are a couple of ways to make the bolt eccentric . The method I used was to bore a .375 hole .110 off center.

Another way to make the eccentric would be to bore the .375 hole in the bolt on center and machine the shaft eccentric.

A 4-jaw chuck can be used to adjust the bolt off center for the drill operation. A 3-jaw chuck could also be used by placing a scrap of 3/32" stock in one jaw.

Face off or cut the end of the bolt off so that the shaft is .50 in length.

Remove the bolt from the chuck and change to a 3 jaw chuck. Mount the shaft end of the bolt in the 3 jaw chuck and face off the head of the bolt to a width of .1875.

**LOWER BLADE GUIDE ASSEMBLY:** The lower base holds the blade guide rollers and is also the mounting platform for the saw table.

Make the base from a piece of 3" channel 3-1/2" long. See fig. 102 for a drawing of the base.

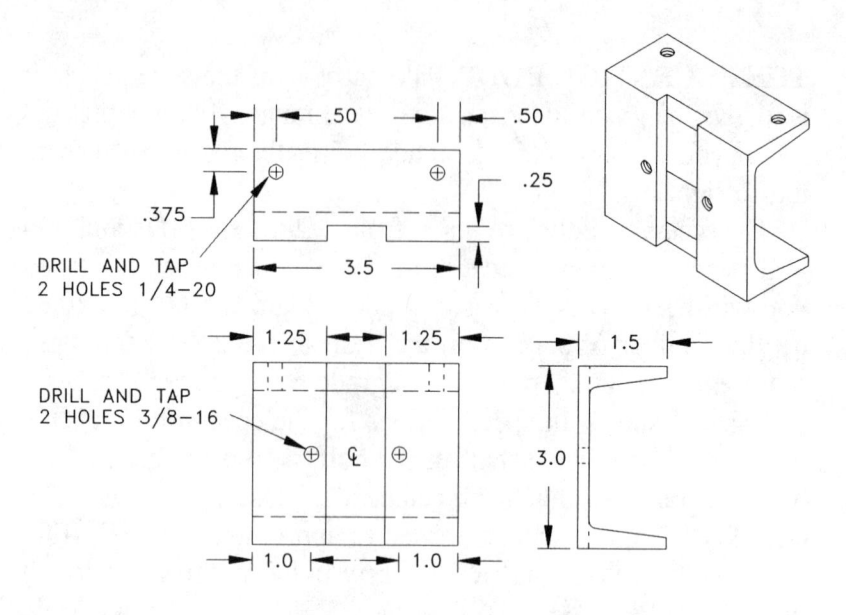

**Figure 102**    **The lower blade guide mounting base**

The 1" wide cut out shown in the center of the base allows clearance for the rear roller guide.

Drill and tap the two 3/8-16 holes in the front of the base for the front guide rollers.

Drill and

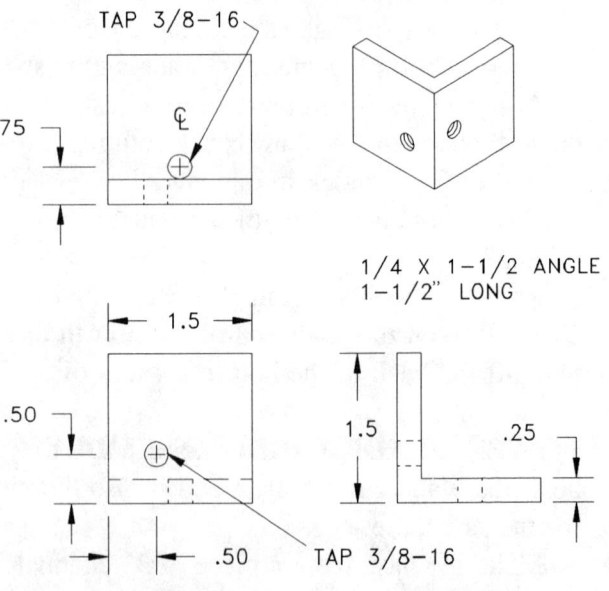

**Figure 103**   **Rear roller guide mounting bracket**

124

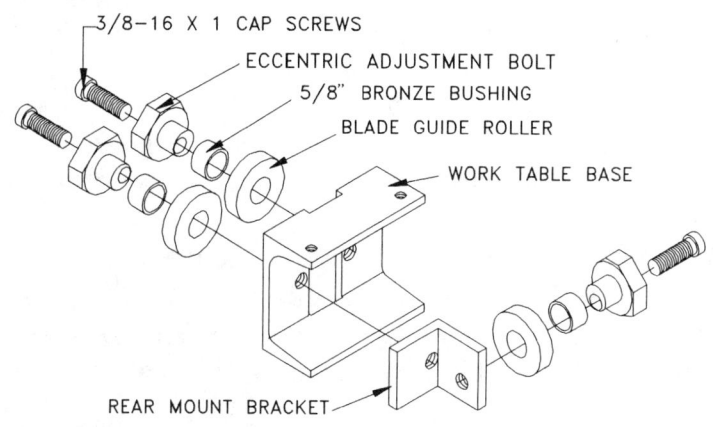

```
     ┌─3/8-16 X 1 CAP SCREWS
     │    ┌─ECCENTRIC ADJUSTMENT BOLT
     │    │    5/8" BRONZE BUSHING
     │    │    BLADE GUIDE ROLLER
     │    │         │    ┌─WORK TABLE BASE
```

**Figure 104**   **Lower blade guide assembly**

tap two holes 1/4-20 in the top of the base. These are for bolting the saw table to the base.

Make the rear roller guide mounting bracket shown in fig. 103 from a piece of 1-1/2 angle 1-1/2" long. Drill and tap a 3/8-16 hole in one side of the bracket in the location shown. The rear roller guide mounts here. Drill another 3/8-16 hole in the other leg of the bracket. This hole is used to mount the bracket to the base.

Have a look at fig. 104 before putting the lower blade guide assembly together.

Bolt the left front roller to the base.

Bolt the right roller assembly and the rear mount bracket to the base. As you can see from the drawing the same bolt that holds the right roller to the base also fastens the rear bracket to the base.

Mount the rear guide roller to the rear bracket.

The mounting bracket for the lower blade guide base is shown in fig. 105. Make it from a piece of 1/4 x 2 flat bar 4-3/4" long. Drill a 1/4" mounting hole in the location shown. Drill three 1/4" holes in the other end of the bracket. With a round file, remove the material between the holes. This forms a curved slot that will be used to adjust the guide roller assembly.

Notice that one end of the mounting bracket is cut at an angle and has a notch cut in it. Align the notch on the mounting bracket with the notch on the roller base and weld the two together. See fig. 107.

The work table is shown in fig. 106. Make it from a piece of 12 ga. sheet steel measuring 5-1/2 x 3-1/2.

Cut the notch on the left side where shown. The notch keeps the work table from hitting the base of the saw when it is

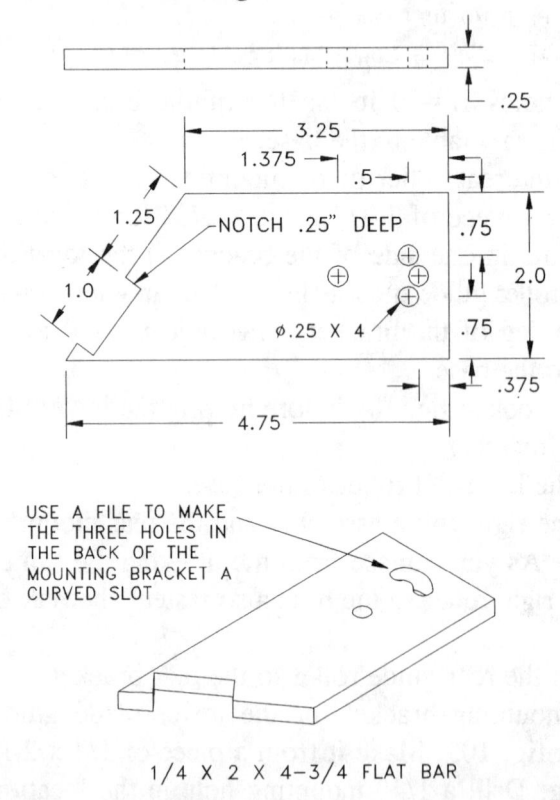

**Figure 105**     **Mounting bracket for the lower guide roller assembly**

cutting in the horizontal position.

The 3/16" wide slot cut 1-1/2" into the work table is for saw blade clearance. Drill two 1/4" holes in the saw table at the locations shown. Counter sink the holes 1/2". The work table is mounted to the base using these holes.

Mount the table to the guide roller base with two 1/4-20 x 1/2 socket head counter sink bolts. See fig. 107.

Bolt the completed guide assembly to the top brace on the lower section vertical frame. Use 1/4-20 x 1 bolts with nuts and lock washers. See Fig. 108.

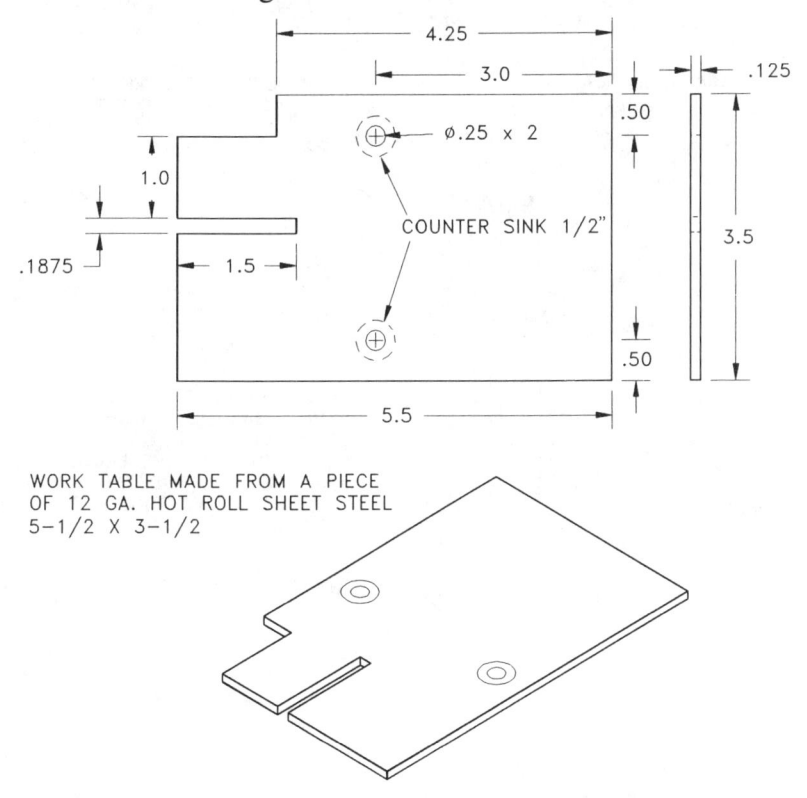

**Figure 106**           **Work table**

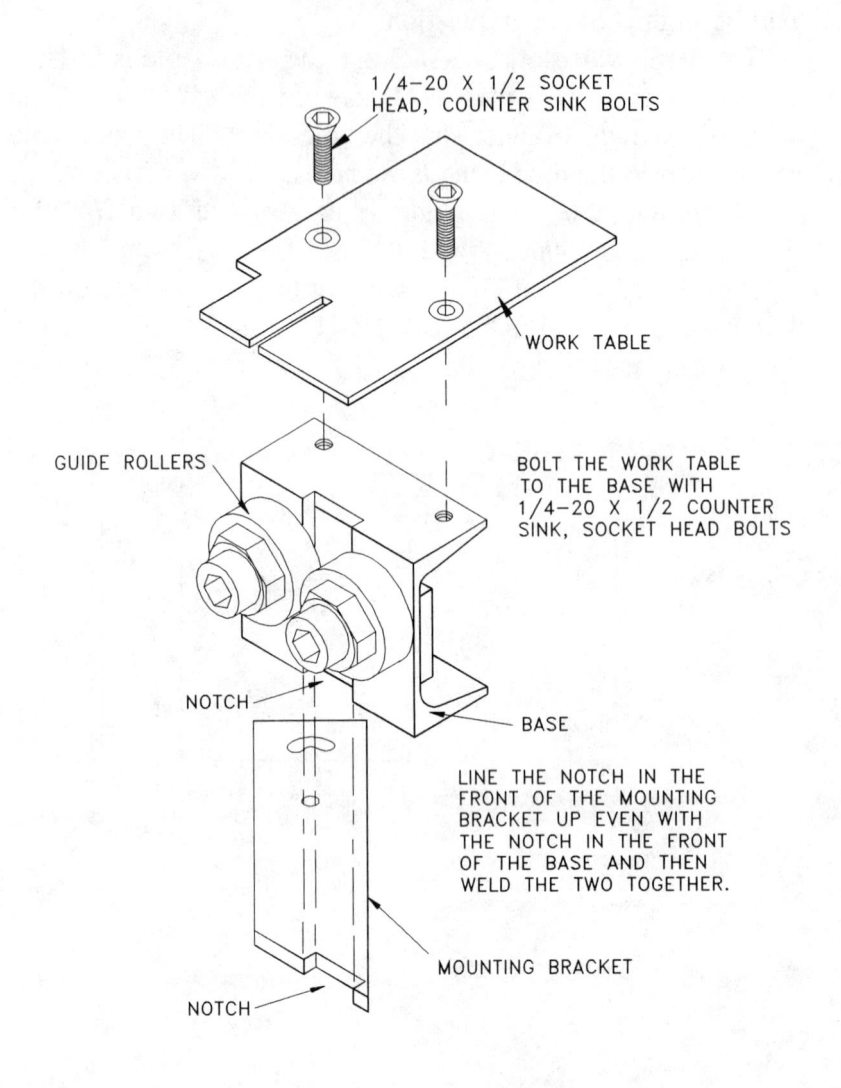

**Figure 107** Bolting the work table to the top of the base, and welding the mounting bracket to the bottom of the base

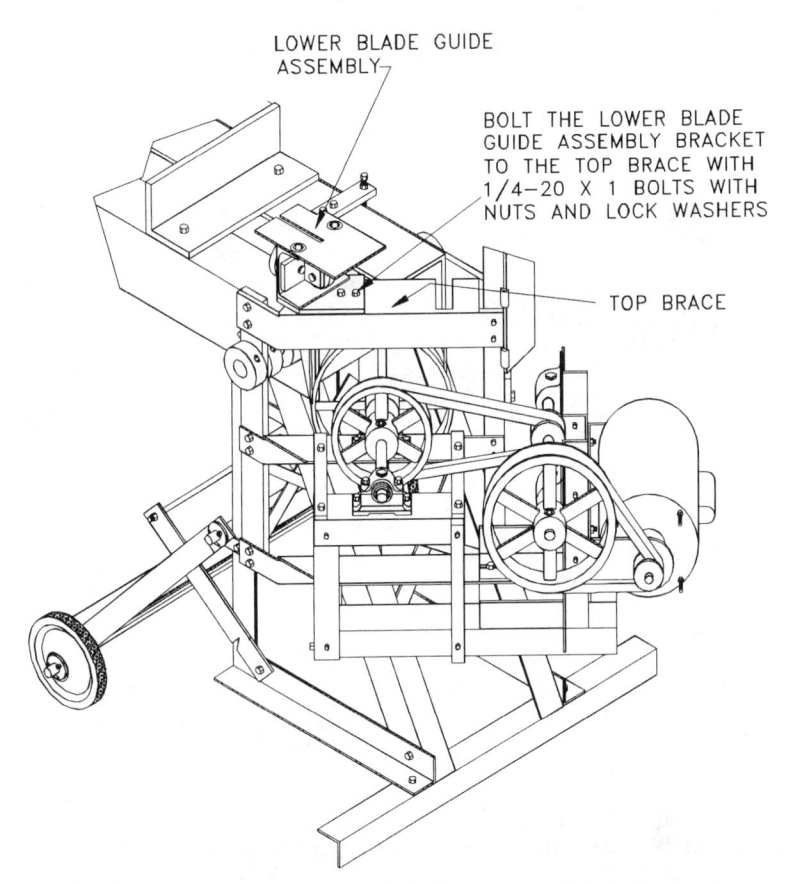

**Figure 108** Mounting the lower blade guide assembly to the top brace

**THE UPPER BLADE GUIDE ASSEMBLY:** The upper blade guide assembly serves the same purpose as the lower blade guide assembly.

The principle operating difference is that the lower blade guide assembly is stationary while the upper assembly adjusts up and down to accommodate different sizes of work.

Make the mounting plate for the upper blade guide assembly from a piece of 1/4 x 4 flat bar 4-1/2" long. Drill the three 1/4" holes in the locations shown in fig. 109.

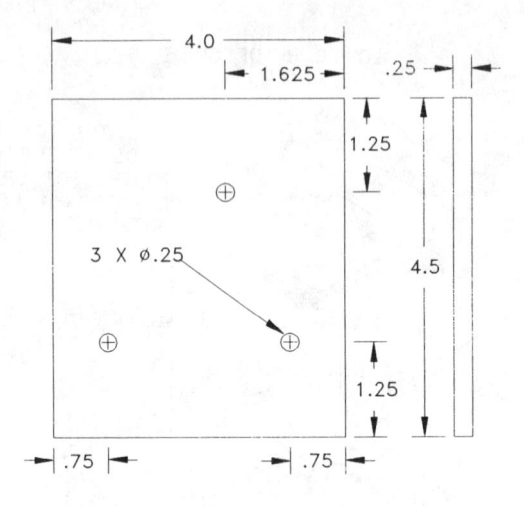

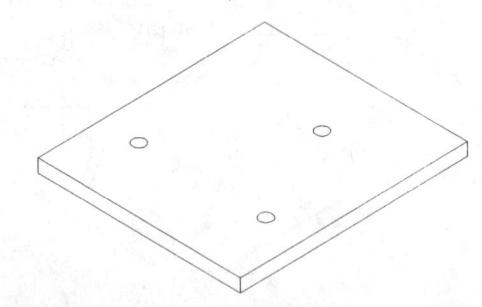

**Figure 109** Mounting plate for the upper blade guide assembly

The mounting base for the upper blade guide rollers is shown in fig. 110. Make it from a piece of 1/4 x 1-1/2 angle 3-1/2" long.

Drill two 1/4" holes in the top of the base in the locations shown. The mounting plate is bolted to the base using these holes.

Drill and tap the two 3/8-16 holes in the front of the base for the front guide rollers.

The 1" wide notch cut in the front of the base is for blade clearance.

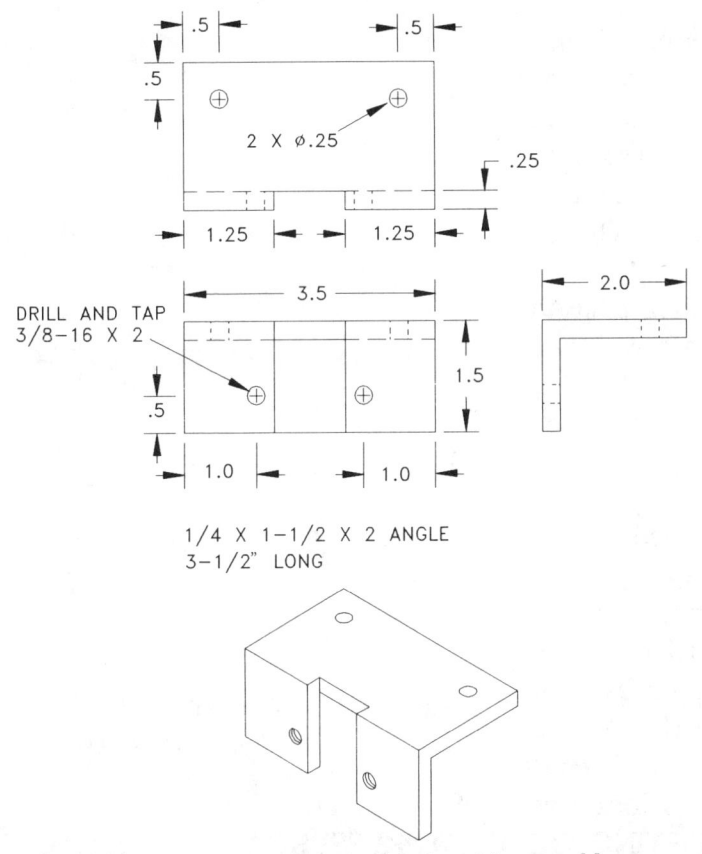

**Figure 110**   Base for the upper blade guide assembly

The rear guide roller mounting bracket is shown in figure 111. Make it from a piece of 1/8 x 1-1/2 angle 1" long. Drill and tap the 3/8-16 hole in the location shown. The rear guide roller mounts here.

A blow up drawing of the upper blade guide assembly is shown in fig. 112. Study it before putting the assembly together.

Weld the rear roller guide bracket to the underside of the base as shown.

Bolt the rear guide roller to the bracket with a 1/4-20 x 1

socket head bolt.

Bolt two guide rollers to the front of the base with the 1/4-20 x 1 socket head bolts.

Bolt the mounting plate to the base with two 1/4-20 x 1 bolts, nuts and lock washers.

Bolt the completed blade guide roller assembly to the adjustable arm on the upper frame of the saw. Use a 1/4-20 x 1 bolt, nut and lock washer. See Fig. 113.

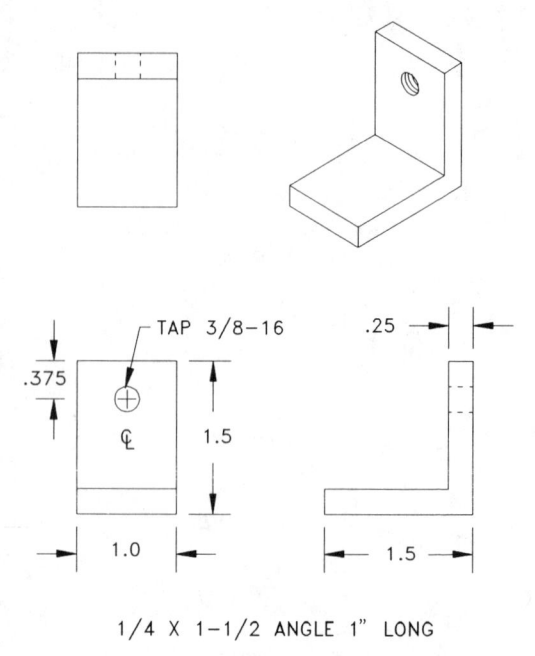

**Figure 111**    Rear guide roller mounting bracket

**MOUNTING THE FEED PRESSURE CONTROL SPRING:**
The feed pressure control spring comes into play when using the saw for horizontal cutting. It controls the rate of descent of the vertical frame and the amount of weight put on the work. Tightening the spring causes a slower descent of the vertical frame and less weight on the work.

Loosening the spring causes a faster descent of the frame putting more weight on the work.

Too much weight causes the blade to twist and jam in the work. Too little weight cause the blade not to cut at all.

Before attaching the spring assembly to the saw, take a look at fig. 114.

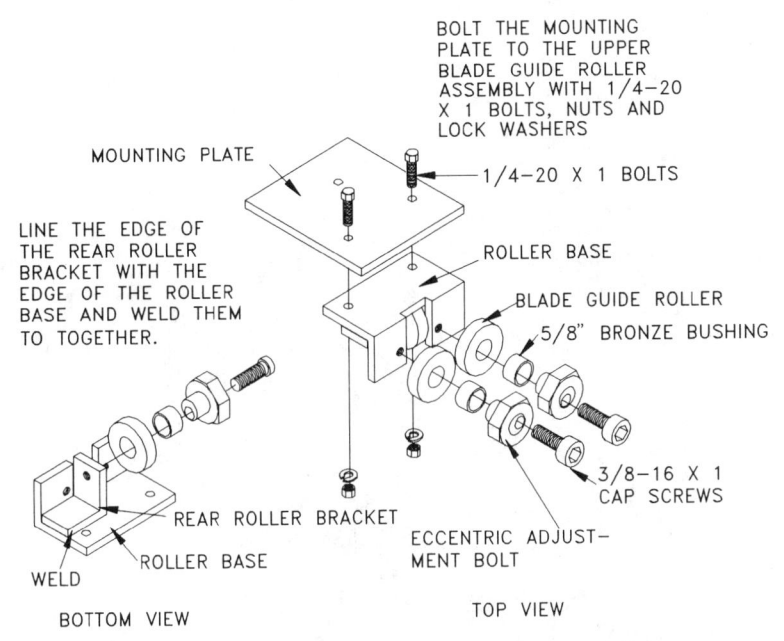

**Figure 112** Blow up drawing of upper blade guide assembly

You can make the spring out of a 150 pound garage door spring. Springs rated less than 150 pounds are not strong enough and those rated greater than 150 are too strong. The best place to find a spring is from a local lumber yard or hardware store. You may also be able to find a used one a lot cheaper in the junk pile of a local garage door installer.

The spring needs to have 9" of coil length. Your spring will no doubt be longer than that, so it will be necessary to cut it to length. The spring is made of hardened steel and a saw blade will not cut it. The best way to cut it is with a torch.

After the spring is cut, form a mounting loop on the cut end to match the loop on the other end. You will have to use heat to form the loop. Heat an area of the spring a couple of coils

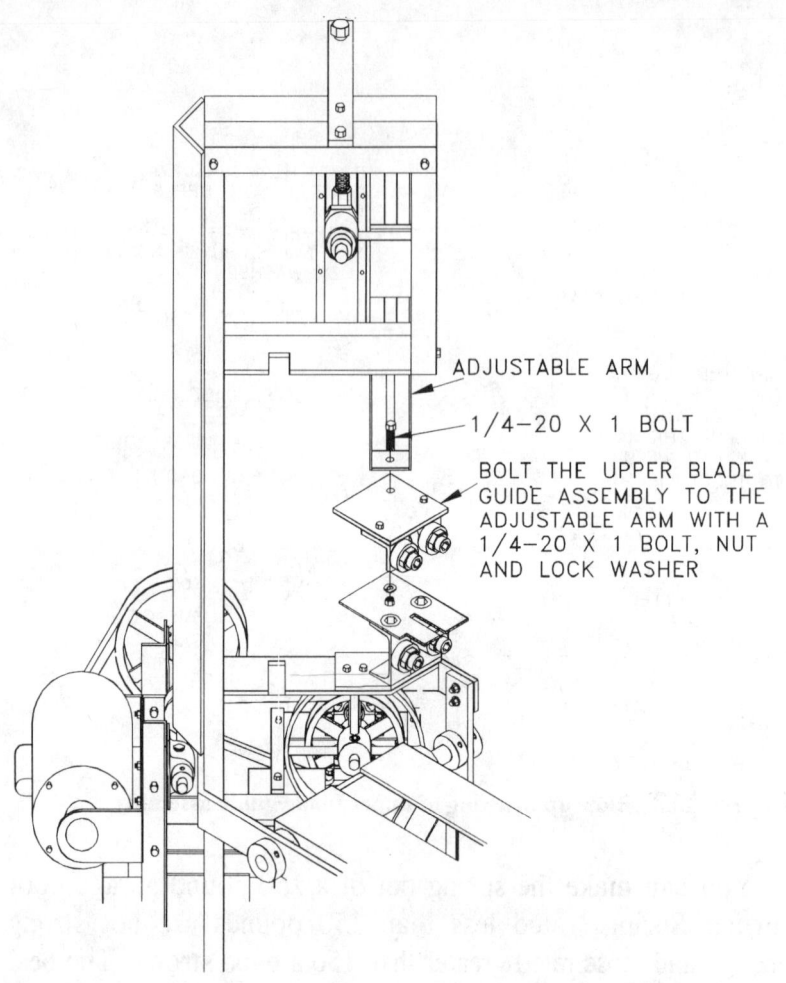

**Figure 113**    Mounting the upper blade guide roller assembly

from the end to a bright red. Heating the spring makes it easy to bend. Form the loop using a pair of pliers.

A 4" turn buckle is used to adjust the tension of the spring. Bolt one end of the turn buckle to the left side pivot arm with a 3/8-16 x 1-1/2 bolt, two nuts and a flat washer. The other end of the turn buckle hooks to the spring. See fig. 114. Turnbuckles of this type are available at most hardware stores.

A 7/8 x 2-3/4 "S" hook is placed on the other end of the

spring and connects the spring to a 1" eye bolt with a 3/8-16 x 2 shank located on the left front leg of the saw.

To install the 1" eye bolt in the left front leg, drill a 3/8" hole in the leg at the location shown in fig. 114. Fasten the eye bolt to the leg with two nuts, one on each side of the leg.

THE TURN BUCKLE IS BOLTED TO THE PIVOT ARM WITH A 3/8-16 X 1-1/2 BOLT. THE BOLT IS SECURED WITH A NUT ON EACH SIDE OF THE PIVOT ARM

3/8-16 X 1-1/2 BOLT, 3/8 FLAT WASHER AND LOCK NUT

THE RING HOOK IS SECURED WITH A 3/8-16 NUT ON EACH SIDE OF THE LEFT FRONT LEG.

PIVOT ARM

10" TURN BUCKLE

150 LB. GARAGE DOOR SPRING CUT DOWN TO 9" IN LENGTH

7/8 X 2-3/4 "S" HOOK

1" EYE BOLT

DRILL A 3/8" HOLE IN THE LEFT LEG, 1/2" DOWN FROM THE BOTTOM EDGE OF THE TABLE

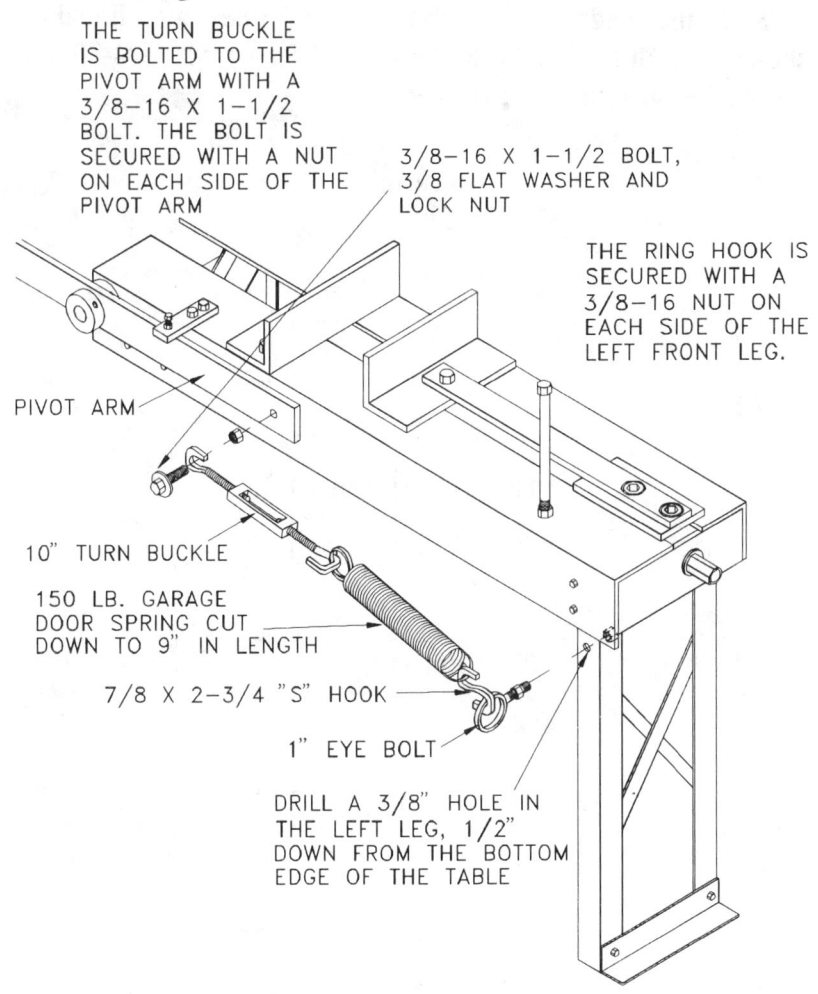

**Figure 114**   Mounting the feed pressure control spring

**MAKING A HANDLE FOR THE VERTICAL FRAME:**
You can buy a handle or you can make one for the vertical frame from a piece of 1/4 x 3/4 flat bar 12" long. If you decide to make a handle refer to fig. 115 for a drawing.

Make the bends in a vise and drill 1/4" holes in each end as shown. Attach the handle to the vertical frame with 1/4-20 x 1 bolts with nuts and lock washers.

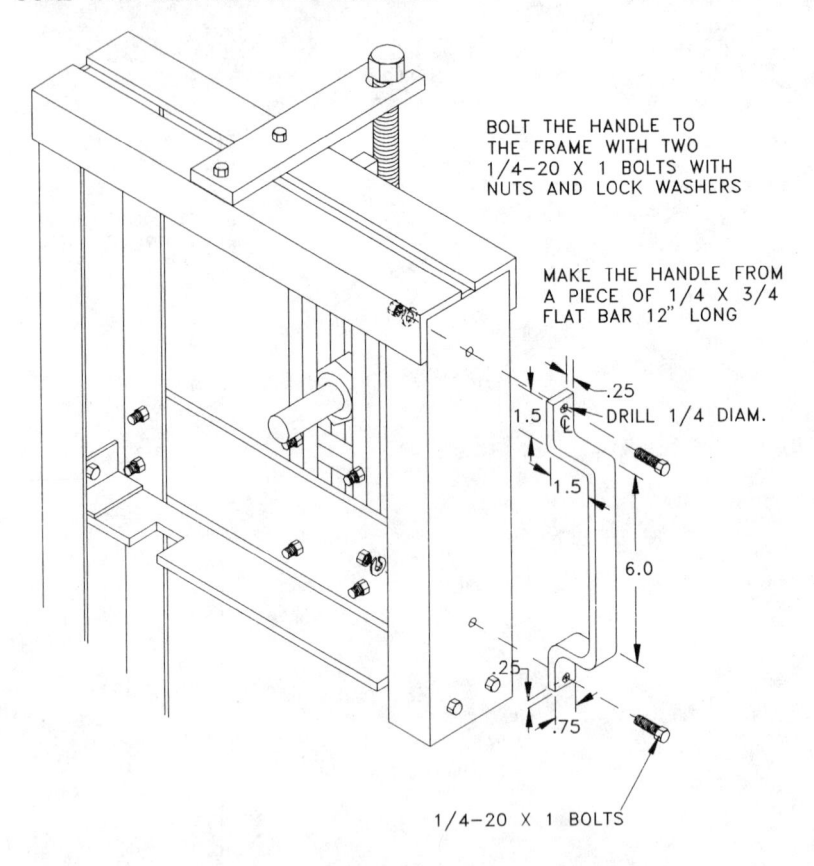

**Figure 115**   Making a handle and bolting it to the vertical frame

**MAKING THE BLADE COVERS:** When the blade comes off the wheels when the saw is in operation it has a tendency to jump away from the frame. It acts kind of like an uncoiling spring. Obviously if this were to happen it could cause personal injury or at the very least damage the blade. For this reason it is important to keep the blade contained.

You can make a door to enclose the idler wheel

THE DOOR IS HELD SHUT BY A 1/4-20 X 1/2 BOLT

DRILL AND TAP 1/4-20

DRILL 1/4

1/4-20 X 1/2 BOLT

DRILL AND TAP SIX #10-24 HOLES IN DOOR FOR THE HINGES

MAKE A DOOR FROM 11-1/2 X 14 12 GAUGE SHEET METAL

#10-24 X 1/2 COUNTER SINK SCREWS

DRILL AND TAP 6 HOLES #10-24

ATTACH THE DOOR TO THE FRAME WITH TWO 3" UTILITY HINGES

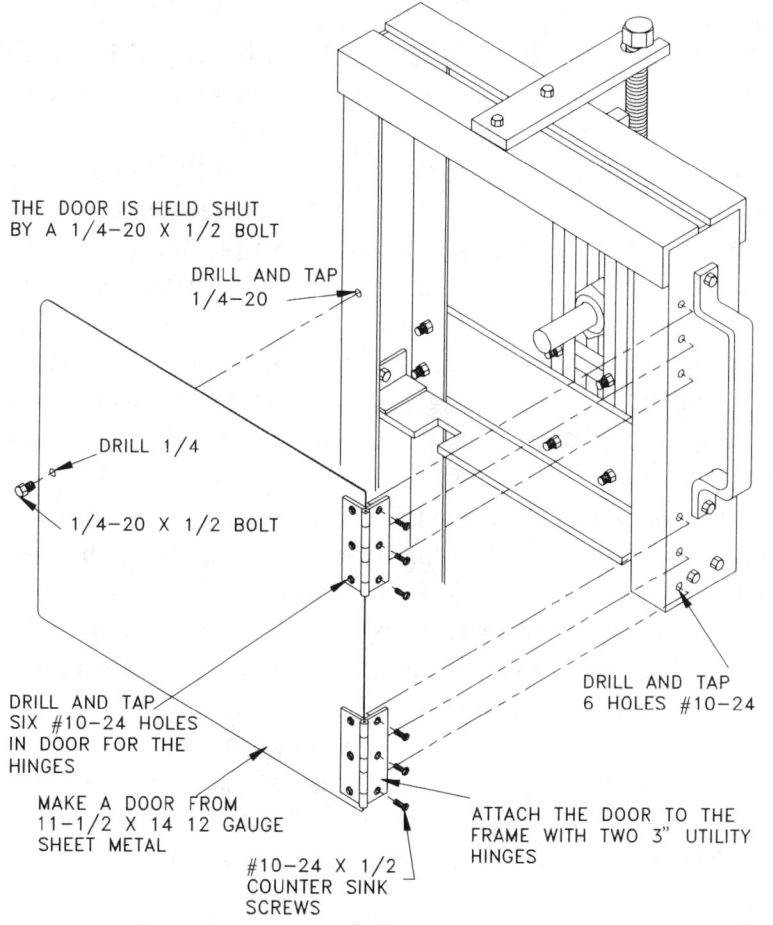

**Figure 116** Making and attaching the door that encloses the idler wheel compartment

compartment. Fig. 116 contains a drawing of the door and how it is mounted. I made my door from a piece of 12 gauge sheet metal measuring 11-1/2 x 14. I did not have a metal shear so I had to cut the door to size using a hand saber saw with a metal cutting blade. You could use a lighter material for the door. Just remember that it must be strong enough to contain the blade and be securely mounted so that it won't fly open while the saw is being used.

To reduce the risk of injury that can be caused by sharp edges, be sure and round the corners on the door and remove any rough or sharp edges on the sheet metal.

As you can see from the drawing, two 3" utility hinges were use to fasten the door to the front of the vertical frame. Locate a hinge approximately 1" from each end of the door. Mark the hole locations to match the hinge. Drill and tap the holes for #10-24 screws.

Mount the hinges to the door using #10-24 x 1/2 screws with a countersink head. The screw will extend out the back of the door keeping the door from shutting. So that the door will shut grind the ends of the screws off flush with the door.

Place the door in position on the vertical frame as shown in fig. 116. Clamp it in place and mark the holes for the hinges. Drill and tap holes in the vertical frame for #10-24 x 1/2 screws and then fasten the door to the frame with those screws.

Drill a 1/4" hole in the left side of the door in the approximate location shown in fig. 116.

Close the door and mark the location of the hole in the vertical post matching it with the location of the hole just drilled in the door. Drill and tap the hole 1/4-20.

The door is secured to the rear vertical post with a 1/4-20 x 1/2 bolt.

The box that encloses the center section of the blade on the left side of the saw is shown in figure 117. Since the location of the hinges and mounting holes are not critical exact location measurements are not shown in the drawing.

The cover box consists of a left side cover plate made from a piece of 20 gauge sheet metal measuring 4-1/2 x 19, The left side cover plate is bolted to the rear post cover with three 1/4-20 x 1 bolts with nuts and lock washers. The post cover is made from 2 pieces of 1/8 x 1-1/2 angle 19" long. The 2 pieces of angle are placed together to form a channel. They are skip welded together along the back seam. A door is attached to the

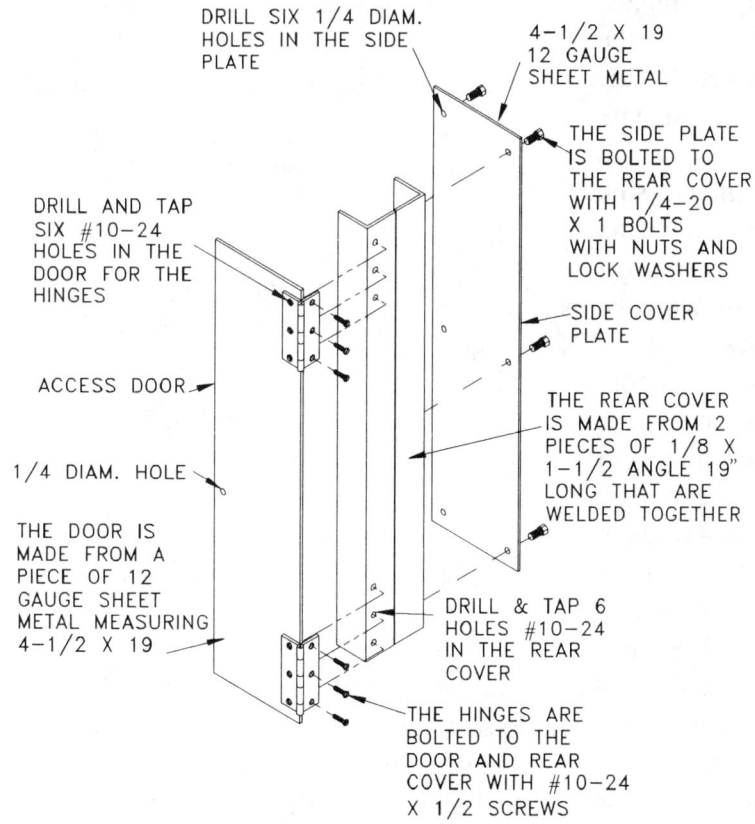

**Figure 117**  Making a box to enclose the rear center portion of the blade

139

other side of the rear post with two 3" utility hinges. The door is made from a piece of 12 gauge sheet metal measuring 4-1/2 x 19.

Drill and tap #10-24 holes in the door and the rear post to match the 3" utility hinges. Mount the hinges to the door and with #10-24 x 1/2 counter sink screws. Grind the screws off flush with the back side of the door. Mount the door hinges to the rear post with #10-24 x 1/2 counter sink screws.

Bolt the left side cover of the box to the vertical post with three 1/4-20 x 1 bolts with nuts and lock washers. The door is secured with a 1/4-20 x 1/2 bolt in the same manner as the idler wheel door. Fig. 118 shows a drawing of the blade covers mounted to the saw frame.

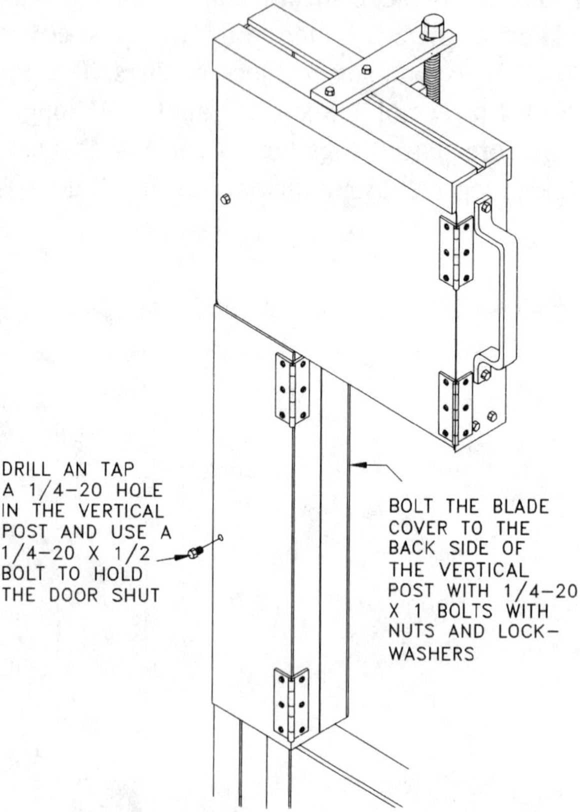

DRILL AN TAP A 1/4-20 HOLE IN THE VERTICAL POST AND USE A 1/4-20 X 1/2 BOLT TO HOLD THE DOOR SHUT

BOLT THE BLADE COVER TO THE BACK SIDE OF THE VERTICAL POST WITH 1/4-20 X 1 BOLTS WITH NUTS AND LOCK-WASHERS

**Figure 118**

**MAKING A COVER FOR THE DRIVE SHAFT:** It's a good idea to make a cover for the drive shaft. This protects the pulleys and bushings from possible damage by falling parts and metal chips. A drawing of the proposed cover and mounting bracket are shown in fig. 119.

Make the cover from a piece of 20 gauge sheet metal measuring 11-1/2 x 11-1/2. Make the bends as shown. The 1/2" tab along the left edge strengthens the cover and also hides the sharp edge.

DRILL A 1/4" HOLE 1/4" FROM THE END OF THE BRACKET

2.0

1.5   1.0

MAKE THE BRACKET FROM 1/8 X 1/1-2 X 2 ANGLE 1" LONG

BRACKET FOR MOUNTING THE COVER

1.5

11.0

DRILL A 1/4" HOLE AT EACH CORNER

MAKE A 125° BEND AT THIS POINT

6.0

4.0

BEND A 1/2" TAB DOWN 90° ON THE EDGE OF THE COVER

.5

MAKE THE 55° BEND AT THIS POINT

MAKE THE DRIVE SHAFT COVER FROM A PIECE OF 20 GAUGE SHEET METAL MEASURING 11.5 X 11.5

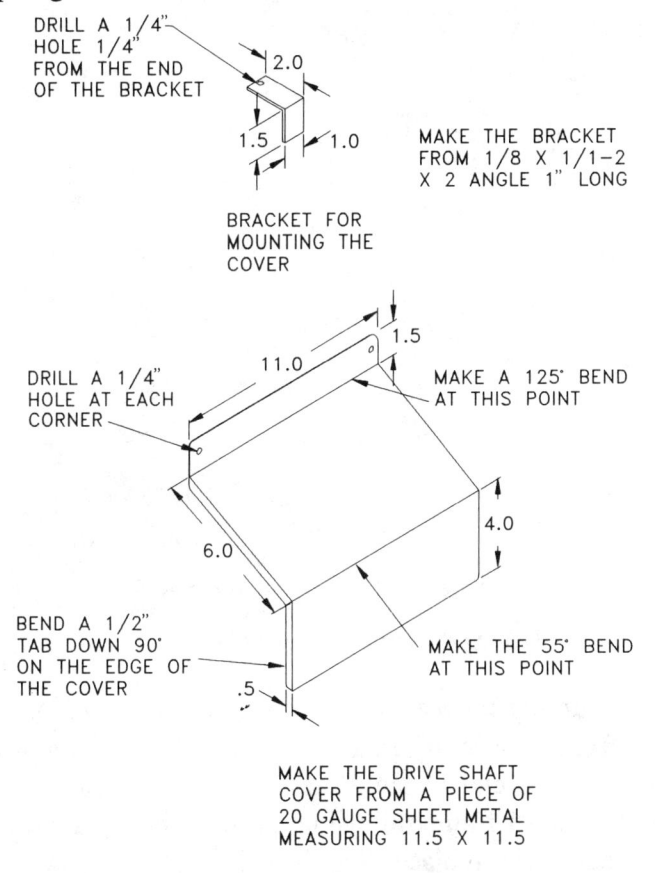

**Figure 119    Making the driveshaft cover and mounting bracket**

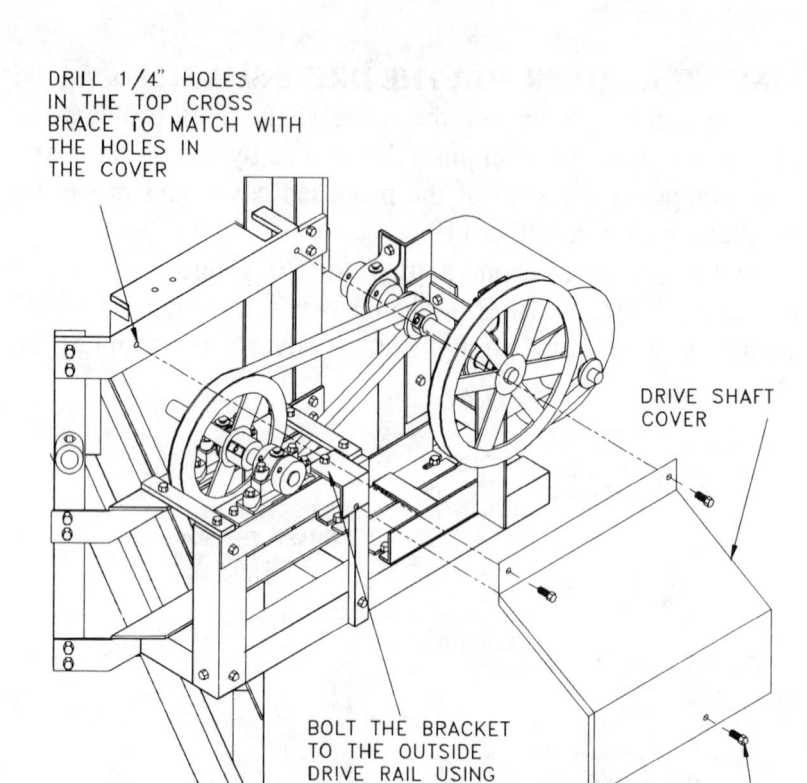

DRILL 1/4" HOLES
IN THE TOP CROSS
BRACE TO MATCH WITH
THE HOLES IN
THE COVER

DRIVE SHAFT
COVER

BOLT THE BRACKET
TO THE OUTSIDE
DRIVE RAIL USING
THE BOLT THAT
HOLDS THE SHIM
IN PLACE

1/4-20 X 1/2
BOLTS

BOLT THE DRIVE SHAFT
COVER TO THE TOP CROSS
BRACE AND MOUNTING
BRACKET WITH 1/4-20
X 1/2 BOLTS WITH NUTS
AND LOCK WASHERS

**Figure 120**  Bolting the driveshaft cover in place

The mounting bracket for the cover is shown in fig. 119. Make it from a piece of 1/8 x 1-1/2 x 2 angle 1" long. Drill a 1/4" hole at the end of the 2" leg. Mount the bracket to the outside drive shaft frame rail using the same bolt that holds the pillow block shim in place. See fig. 120.

Bolt the cover in place as shown in fig. 120. Drill a 1/4"

POSITION THE BRACKET ON THE RIGHT FRONT LEG ABOUT 2" BELOW THE BOTTOM EDGE OF THE TABLE TOP AND WELD IT IN PLACE

MAKE A MOUNTING BRACKET OUT OF A PIECE OF 1-1/2 ANGLE 1" LONG

BOLT THE ELECTRICAL BOX TO THE BRACKET WITH A 1/4-20 X 1/2 BOLT WITH NUT AND LOCK WASHER

DRILL A 1/4" HOLE IN THE SIDE OF THE ELECTRICAL BOX AND THE BRACKET.

2-1/8 X 4 STEEL ELECTRICAL OUTLET BOX

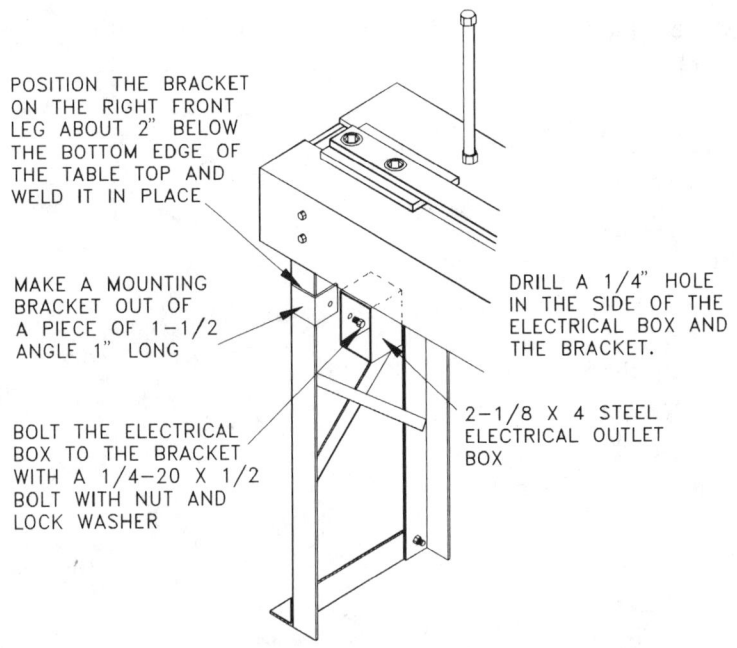

**Figure 121** Mounting the switch box to the right front leg of the saw

hole in each end of the top of the cover and into the side of the top cross brace. Bolt the cover to the cross brace with two 1/4-20 x 1/2 bolts with nuts and lock washers. Drill a 1/4" hole in the bottom of the cover and through the mounting bracket. Bolt the cover to the mounting bracket with a 1/4-20 x 1 x 1/2 bolt with a nut and lock washer.

**THE AUTOMATIC SHUT OFF ASSEMBLY:** The 2-1/8 x 4 steel electrical box for the switch is bolted to a bracket on the right front leg of the saw table. Make the bracket from a piece of 1/8 x 1-1/2 angle 1" long and weld it to the right front leg, 2" below the bottom edge of the saw table. See fig. 121.

The stabilizer bracket and switch bracket for the automatic cut off assembly are shown in fig. 122.

Make the stabilizer bracket from a piece of 1/8 x 1 strap 4-1/2" long. Bend the bracket into a "U" shape as shown in the figure. Drill a 1/4" hole at the end of each leg.

Make the switch bracket from a piece of 1/8 x 1 angle 1" long. Drill and tap a 1/4-20 hole in one leg of the bracket. Drill a 1/4" hole in the other leg of the bracket.

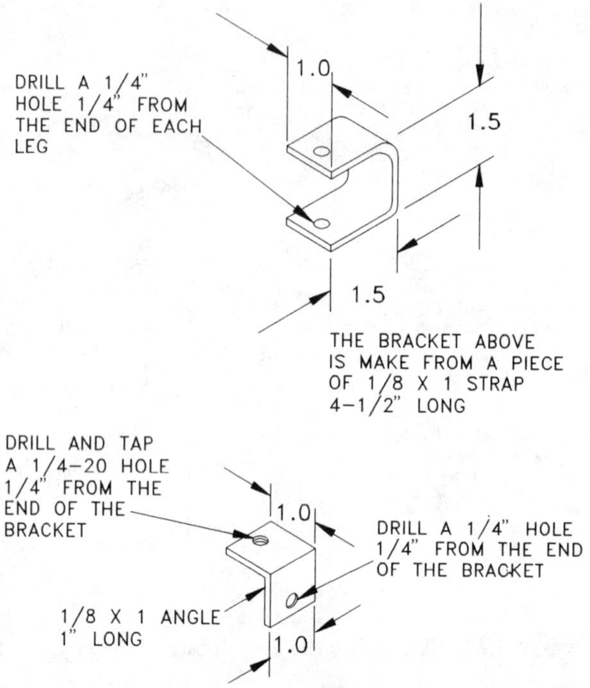

The switch is a heavy duty DPST toggle switch rated at 20 amp 120V AC for a 1-1/2 HP motor. The toggle switch arm is made of metal. The switch cover plate is also made of metal.

Wire and ground the saw properly following the electrical codes in your area. If you are unsure how to do the wiring consult someone who is. Be sure that all wiring is secured with wire ties and is completely out of the way of the saw blade and drive assembly. Also make sure the wire does not get pinched between the saw table and vertical frame when the saw is used in the horizontal position.

A blowup drawing of the automatic shut off assembly is

**Figure 122** The stabilizer and switch brackets for the automatic shut of assembly

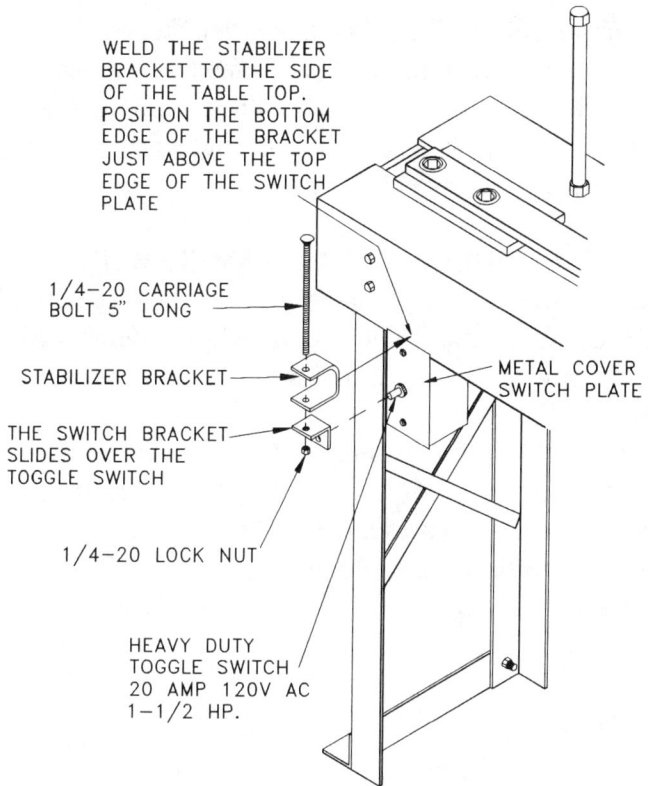

**Figure 123**   The automatic shut off assembly

shown in fig. 123.

Position the stabilizer bracket on the side of the saw table just above the top edge of the switch plate. The holes in the bracket should be aligned with the toggle switch. When the bracket is in position weld it to the table.

Slide the 1/4" hole in the switch bracket over the toggle switch arm. The other leg of the bracket with the threaded hole will face away from the saw.

Insert a 1/4-20 X 5 carriage bolt through the 2 holes in the stabilizer bracket and thread the bolt into the threaded hole in the switch bracket.

The carriage bolt is adjusted so that when the saw blade cuts through a piece of work the vertical frame hits the head of the carriage bolt and shuts the saw off. When the bolt is adjusted properly, secure it with a lock nut tightened against the underneath side of the switch bracket.

**MAKING A HANDLE FOR THE SAW TABLE:** Having a handle on the front of the saw table makes it much easier when you want to engage and disengage the wheel assembly as well as move the saw around. A drawing of the handle assembly is shown in fig. 124.

Make a handle from a 6" length of 1 x 3 square wall tubing and a piece of 1/2" pipe 14" long. The material thickness of the square wall tubing measures about .080.

Cut 1" off one side of the tubing. This leaves a 2" wide "U" shaped bracket 6" long. Drill 1/4" holes in the bracket at the

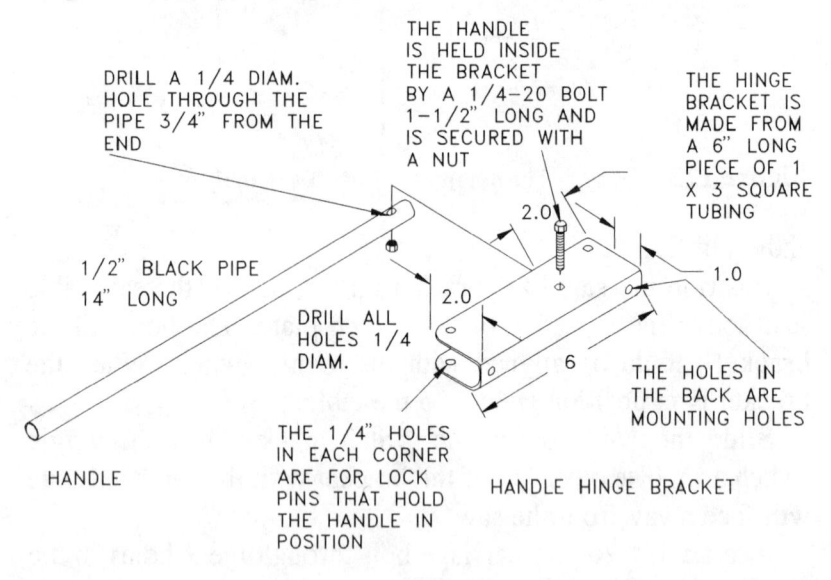

**Figure 124**            **Handle assembly**

146

locations shown. The holes located at the outside corners of the bracket are for pins that lock the handle in position. The holes on the back end of the bracket are for mounting the bracket to the saw frame. The other hole in the top of the bracket is for mounting the handle to the bracket.

Drill a 1/4" hole in the black pipe 3/4" from one end. Set the

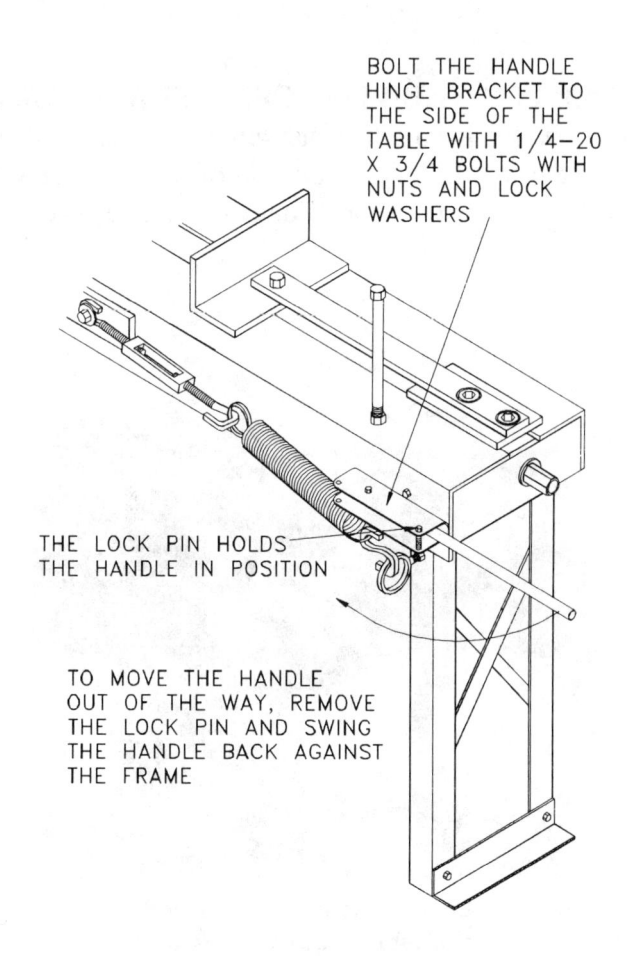

**Figure 125**     Mounting the handle to the saw frame

pipe in the bracket and align the hole in the pipe with the hole in the top of the bracket as shown in fig. 124. Bolt the pipe and bracket together with a 1/4-20 x 1-1/2 bolt and nut.

Locate the handle in the approximate position shown in figure 125. Drill 1/4" holes in the side of the table in line with the holes in the back of the handle bracket. Bolt the bracket to the side of the table with 1/4-20 x 3/4 bolts with nuts and lock washers.

**A HANDLE FOR THE VISE SCREW SHAFT:** We found an old water valve handle that measured 4" across and simply welded it to the coupling nut at the end of the vise screw shaft. Fig. 126 shows what the handle looks like on our saw.

**Figure 126**    Close up showing vise handle and automatic shut off assembly

# THE BLADE WHEELS

**CUTTING THE BLADE WHEEL BLANKS:** Fig. 127 shows a drawing of the blade wheel blank. The blade wheel blanks are cut from 8" I.D. pipe. The actual finished width of the blade wheels will be 1". Notice that the width shown is 1/4" wider than the finished width. The excess will be removed when facing off both ends of the wheel. If you are not very good at cutting a straight line with a torch you may even have to allow more width to the blank. It is important that the blade wheel blanks be cut off as straight as possible. The straighter and more uniform the cut, the easier the finishing process on the lathe will be later.

Using a jig is one way to cut a straight edge when torch cutting a piece of pipe. The jig is a piece of sheet metal cut the length of the circumference of the pipe.

To figure the length of the jig multiply the diameter of the pipe by 3.1416. In the case of our 8" I.D. pipe, its approximate outside diameter is 8.625". Multiply 3.1416 x 8.625" = 27.134". Cut a 2" wide piece of sheet metal 27.134" long.

Wrap the jig

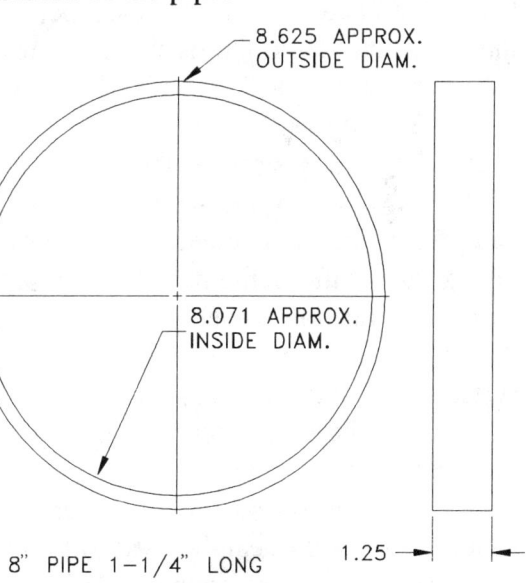

**Figure 127** Blade wheel blank. Make 2

around the pipe at the desired cut point and tape it in position. This will give you a straight edge to mark the burn line with. Mark the line with highly visible chalk and remove the jig. Set the pipe on a non flammable surface and let the cut off end extend out over the edge. Place blocks at each side of the pipe to prevent it from rolling around.

Be sure and take the appropriate safety precautions when using a cutting torch. And always wear protective goggles.

Refer to the manufactures instructions and select the correct size nozzle for cutting. Adjust the oxygen and acetylene pressures at the regulator in accordance with those same instructions. Light the blowpipe and adjust the preheat flame to neutral with the cutting-oxygen valve open.

Hold the blowpipe in your right hand so that you have instant and positive control of the cutting oxygen lever. Steady the blow pipe with your left hand. Hold the nozzle perpendicular to the surface at the top center of the pipe, and about 1/16" behind the chalk line. Hold the torch steady until the spot is raised to a bright red heat and then slowly release the cutting oxygen lever. As soon as the cutting starts there will be a shower of sparks. When this happens, the oxygen lever should be pressed all the way down. Move the blowpipe slowly but steadily to the right following the marked line. Movement should be just fast enough to let the flame penetrate the pipe completely without excessive oxidation or melting. As the cut progresses make sure the cutting head remains perpendicular and follows the curved surface of the pipe. If you stand so you can look down into the cut you will be in a better position to see if you are moving at the proper rate of speed.

To make things somewhat easier, the pipe can be set on rollers and a helper can be used to turn the pipe as the cutting process continues uninterrupted. If a helper is used, make sure he or she adheres to all safety rules.

If the blow pipe is moved too slowly, the edges will tend to melt producing a ragged appearance, or at times fusing the metal together. On the other hand, if it is moved too rapidly the cutting jet will fail to go through the pipe and cutting will be stopped. If cutting stops immediately release the oxygen lever and reheat to a bright red the point where the cut stopped. Open the oxygen valve again and restart the cut.

After the cut is complete it is likely that slag will still hold the pieces together. Give the edge a tap with a hammer and it should separate. Let the work air cool. <u>Do not</u> quench it in cold water. This would cause the metal to harden and make future lathe operations difficult, if not impossible.

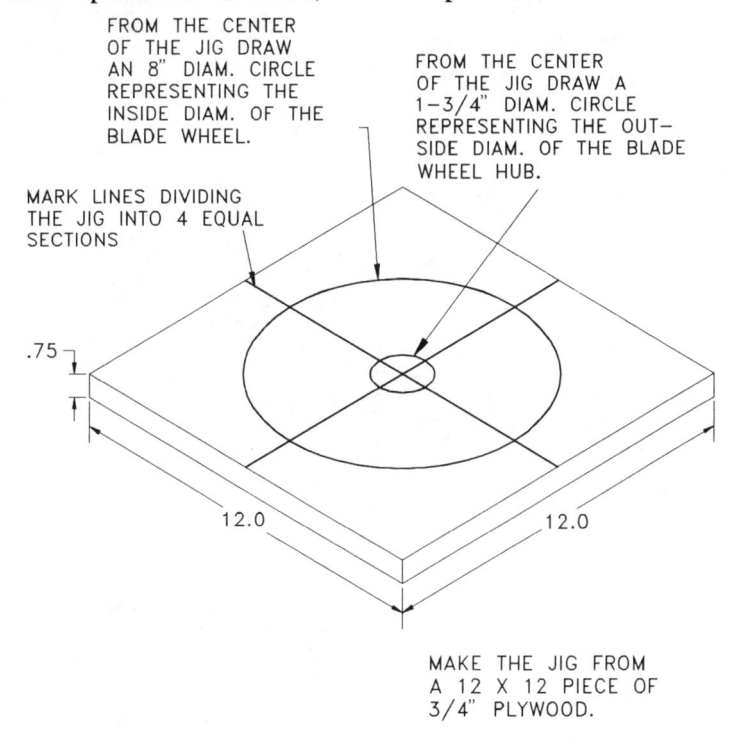

**Figure 128**     **The base for the blade wheel jig**

**MAKING THE BLADE WHEELS:** The drive wheel and idler wheel each consist of a 1-1/4" wide piece of 8" I.D. pipe which is the wheel, a hub that is made from a piece 1-3/4" Dia. round bar stock 1-3/4" long and four spokes made from 3-1/8" long 1/2" round rod. The only difference between the two, is that the idler wheel has a 3/4" bore and the drive wheel has a 5/8" bore.

To avoid a lot of machine work the wheels must be assembled as accurately as possible. This is accomplished by the use of a jig.

The jig is made from a piece of plywood and a few brackets made from angle iron.

The base of the jig is shown in fig. 128. Make it from a

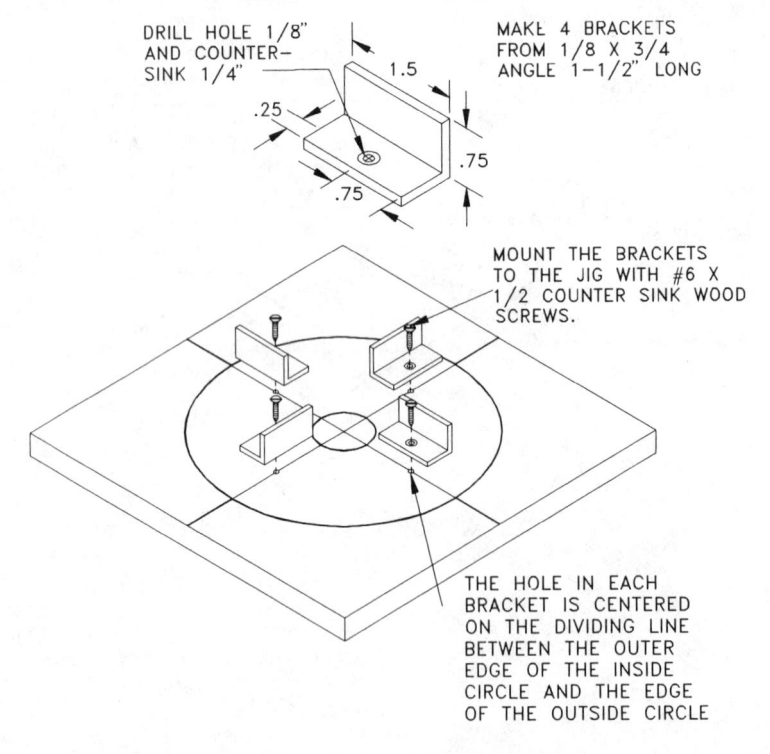

**Figure 129**      **Base mounting brackets. Make 4**

piece of 3/4" plywood 12" x 12".

Locate the center of the jig base and mark lines dividing it into four equal sections. From the center of the jig draw a 1-3/4" circle representing the outside diameter of the blade wheel hub. Also draw an 8" circle representing the inside diameter of the wheel.

Four brackets are mounted to the jig base. They hold the spokes for the blade wheel.

Make the brackets from four pieces of 1/8" x 3/4" angle 1-1/2" long. Drill an 1/8" hole in each of them as shown in fig. 129. Counter sink each hole 1/4".

Center a bracket on each of the 4 dividing lines between the 1-3/4" inner circle and the 8" outer circle. Mount the brackets to the jig base with #6 x 1/2" counter sink wood screws.

The drawing of the blade wheel hub is shown in fig. 130.

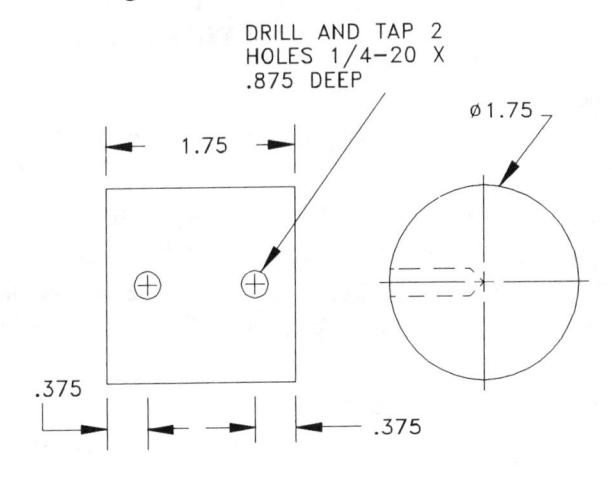

1-3/4" DIAM. ROUND ROD

**Figure 130**     **Blade wheel hub. Make 2**

Make it from a piece of 1-3/4" dia. round rod 1-3/4" long. Drill and tap a 1/4-20 hole 7/8" deep and 3/8" from each end of the hub. The holes are for the set screws. It is best to use a "V" block when drilling and tapping round rod.

Mount one of the wheel hubs in a 3 jaw chuck on the lathe and face off one end. When finished remove it from the lathe and place the faced off end on the jig base. Align the outside edge of the hub with the 1-3/4" circle on the jig. see fig. 132.

**Figure 131** Facing off the blade wheel

The slag and rough edges left by the cutting torch will dull the cutting tool on a lathe in a hurry. For this reason it is best to grind the slag and rough edges off the blade wheel before mounting it in the lathe. A disk grinder is best for this kind of work.

Mount a blade wheel blank in a 4-jaw chuck on the lathe. Center it in the chuck and face off the end. See fig. 131.

When finished remove the blade wheel blank from the lathe and set the faced off end on the jig base. Line up the inside edge of the wheel with the 8" circle on the base. See fig. 132.

Next make 8 spokes for the blade wheels. Each wheel requires 4. Make them from 1/2" round rod approximately 3-1/8" long. It is best to cut them a little longer than needed and then custom fit each one using a bench grinder to grind off the excess.

Before placing the spokes on the jig make 4 spacers from 1/8" x 1-1/2" strap iron 1/2" long.

Place a spacer on each of the brackets located on the jig. Place the spokes on top of the spacers. See fig. 133.

Each spoke is held in place with a clamp bracket. Four clamps are required. Make them from 1/8" x 3/4" angle 1-1/2"

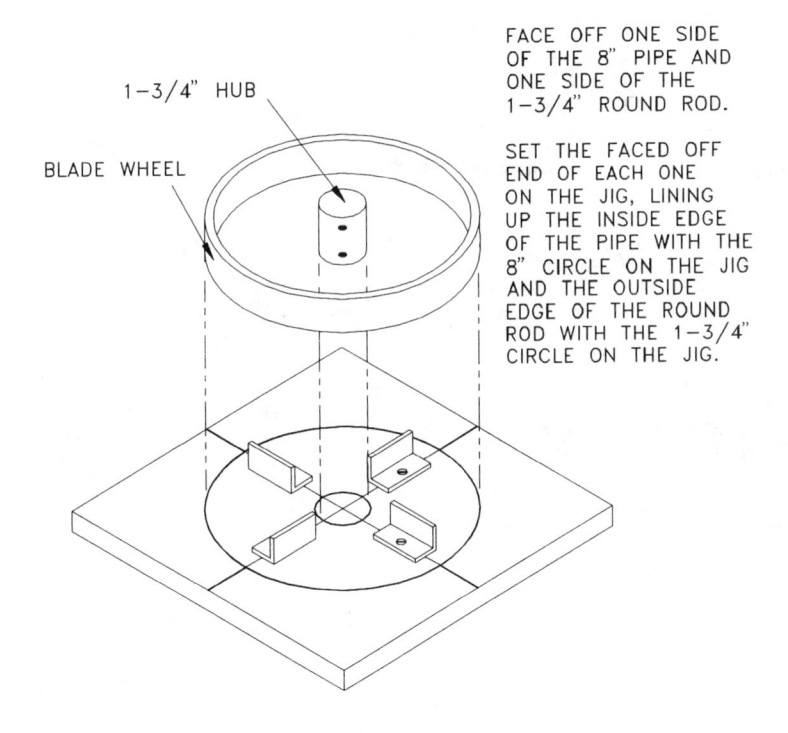

```
1-3/4" HUB

BLADE WHEEL

FACE OFF ONE SIDE
OF THE 8" PIPE AND
ONE SIDE OF THE
1-3/4" ROUND ROD.

SET THE FACED OFF
END OF EACH ONE
ON THE JIG, LINING
UP THE INSIDE EDGE
OF THE PIPE WITH THE
8" CIRCLE ON THE JIG
AND THE OUTSIDE
EDGE OF THE ROUND
ROD WITH THE 1-3/4"
CIRCLE ON THE JIG.
```

**Figure 132**   Placing the hub and blade wheel blank on the jig base

CUT FOUR SPACERS
1/8 X 1/2 X 1-1/2

CUT 4 SPOKES
3-1/8" LONG
FROM 1/2"
ROUND ROD

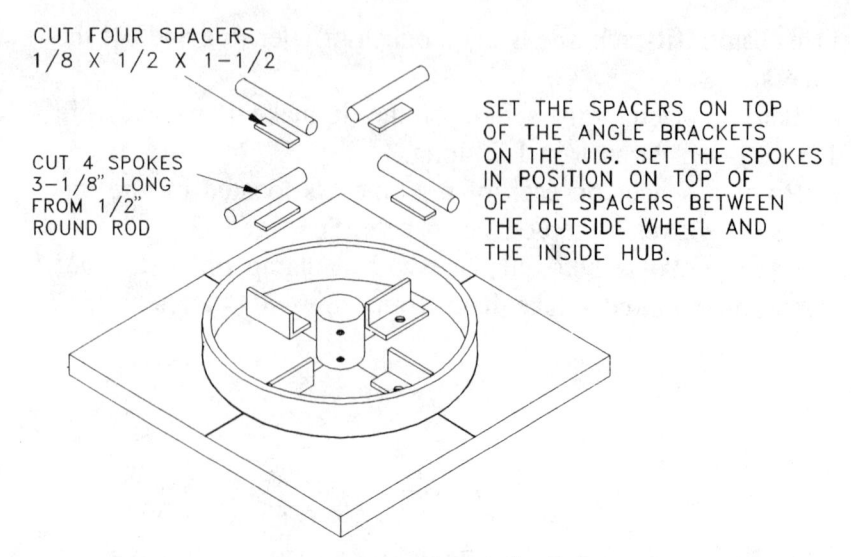

SET THE SPACERS ON TOP OF THE ANGLE BRACKETS ON THE JIG. SET THE SPOKES IN POSITION ON TOP OF OF THE SPACERS BETWEEN THE OUTSIDE WHEEL AND THE INSIDE HUB.

**Figure 133**  Placing the spokes on the jig base

1/4 X 1-1/4 LAG SCREWS

DRILL 1/4"
.75
.75
1.5
.25

CLAMP THE SPOKES IN PLACE BY SCREWING THE CLAMP BRACKETS TO THE BASE OF THE JIG.

MAKE 4 CLAMP BRACKETS FROM 1/8 X 3/4 ANGLE 1-1/2" LONG

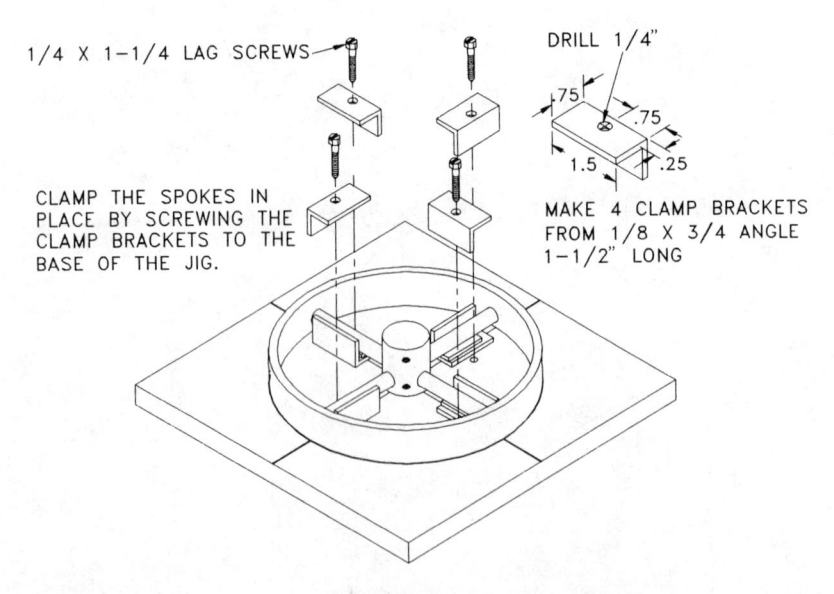

**Figure 134**  Clamping the spokes in place

long. Drill a 1/4" hole in each clamp in the location shown in fig. 134.

Clamp the spokes in place by screwing the clamp brackets to the base of the jig in the locations shown in fig. 134.

Make 4 clamp brackets from 1/8" x 1" angle 1-1/2" long. Drill a 1/4" hole in each bracket where shown. These brackets are used to hold the blade wheel on the jig. They are held in place with 1/4" x 2" lag bolts. See fig. 135.

After every thing is in position weld the spokes to the blade wheel and the hub. I used 6013 welding rod and set my welder on about 70 amps to do the job. Be sure and protect the threaded holes in the hub from weld splatter. There is a possibility that the wooden jig could catch on fire so keep a bucket of water handy.

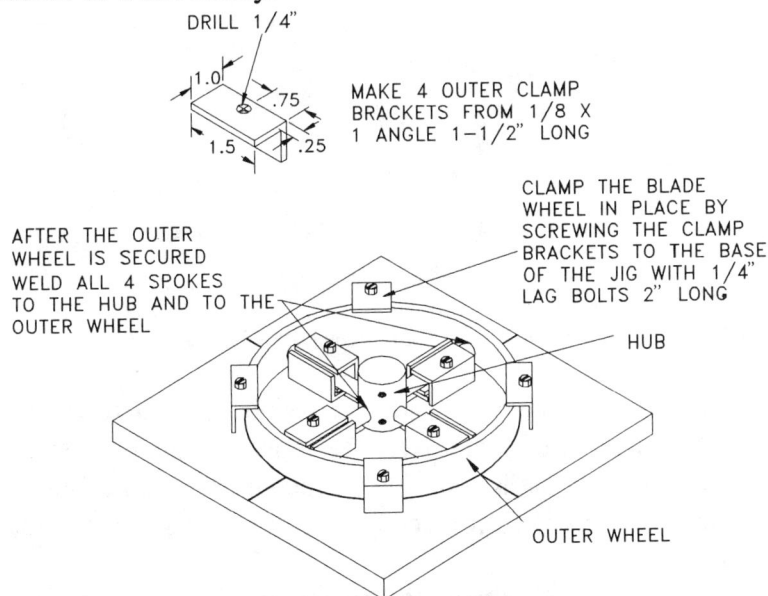

**Figure 135**     **Clamping the outer wheel to the jig and welding the spokes in place**

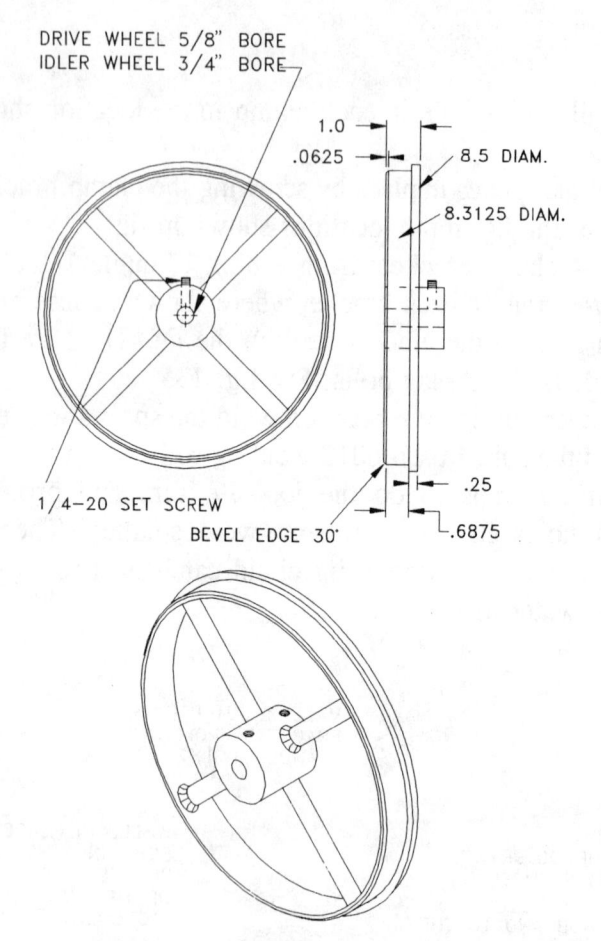

**Figure 136**    **Blade wheel dimensions**

When the top side of the spokes have been welded, remove the wheel from the jig and weld the spokes on the back side.

When the welding is complete set the wheel on a flat surface and let it air cool. If you set it on an uneven surface it may warp.

While the wheel is cooling you can make the second wheel by repeating the previous steps.

There are several ways to set up the blade wheel for the necessary machine work. One way, and probably the best, is to bore the hole in the hub as close to center as possible. It is best to bore to near size and finish with a reamer.

Insert the set screws in the hub and mount the wheel on an arbor for the remainder of the machine work required.

Turn the surface of the wheel and face off both ends following the dimensions in fig. 136.

**Figure 137**

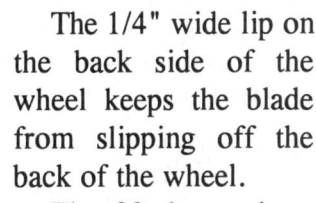

**Figure 138**

The 1/4" wide lip on the back side of the wheel keeps the blade from slipping off the back of the wheel.

The 30 degree beveled edge on the wheel allows clearance for the blade teeth. Without the beveled edge, the teeth on the saw blade would flatten against the wheel and loose their set.

Both blade wheels are made exactly the same. The only difference between the two is that the idler wheel is bored 3/4", and the drive wheel is bored 5/8".

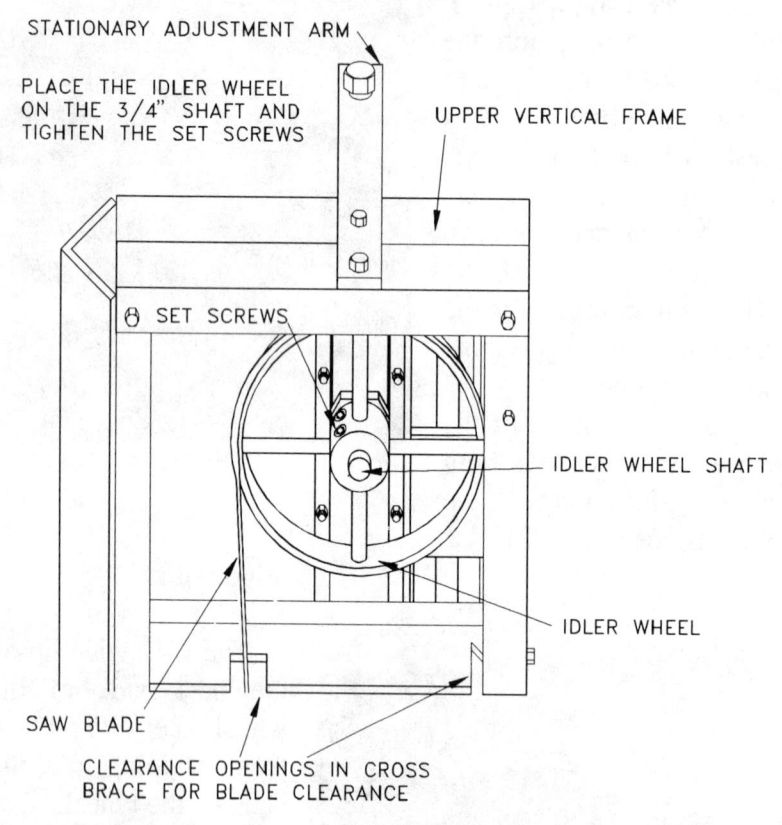

**Figure 139**     Mounting the idler wheel

**MOUNTING THE BLADE WHEELS:** Mount the idler wheel on the 3/4" idler shaft and mount the drive wheel on the 5/8" drive shaft. Tighten the set screws. See figures 139 and 140.

THE PITCH DIRECTION OF THE TEETH ON THE SAW BLADE MUST POINT IN THE DIRECTION THE SAW BLADE TRAVELS

THE SAW BLADE TRAVELS IN THIS DIRECTION

SAW BLADE

SET SCREWS

DRIVE WHEEL

DRIVE SHAFT

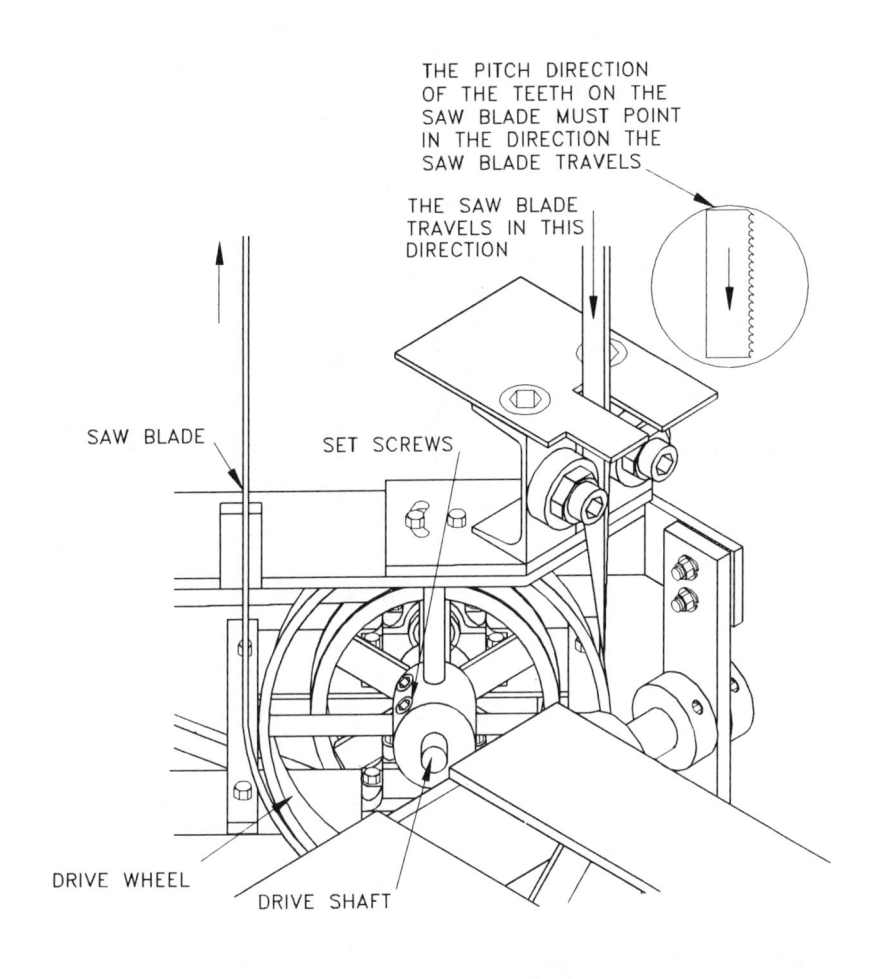

PLACE THE DRIVE WHEEL ON THE DRIVE SHAFT AND TIGHTEN THE SET SCREWS.

**Figure 140**          **Mounting the lower blade wheel**

**MOUNTING THE SAW BLADE:** The saw blade I used measures 94", is 3/4" wide, .035 thick and has 14 teeth per inch. The tooth set is raker and the blade type is carbon flex back. Most industrial supply houses carry bandsaw blades. To

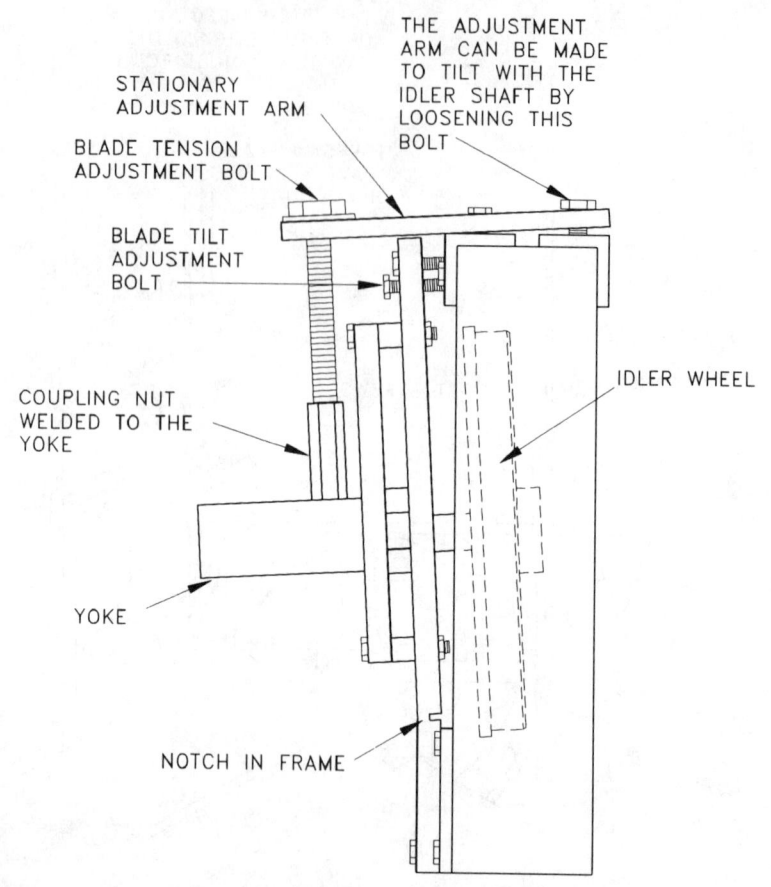

**Figure 141**   Adjusting the blade tension and tracking

order blades It's a good idea to call them ahead of time. When I order blades they usually have them ready the next day. The 14 tooth blade is suitable for most jobs including aluminum. A 10 tooth blade would cut heavy sections faster and a 24 tooth blade would be preferable for cutting tubing.

If you plan to do a lot of cutting you might consider one the Bi-Metal type blades. They cost about twice as much as the carbon flex back blades, but they last about 10 times longer. They are also welded together much better which reduces the chance of the blade breaking. I am using one on my saw for the first time and am very happy with its performance. Place the bandsaw blade over both blade wheels. The pitch angle of the blade teeth should point in a downward direction or in this case the same direction as the blade travels.

Thread the blade through the upper and lower guide rollers. Figures 139 and 140 show how the blade looks as it goes through the clearance openings in the upper frame cross brace and the lower frame cross brace. The drawing also shows how the blade looks as it goes through the lower blade guide rollers.

**ADJUSTING THE BLADE:** For efficient and accurate cutting, the guide rollers must be adjusted so that they hold the blade perpendicular to the work, and guide the blade straight without bending or allowing it to sag between the rollers.

Tighten the blade tension using the blade tension adjustment bolt shown in fig. 141. Tighten it just enough to pick up the slack.

The first chore is to line the idler wheel up with the drive wheel. Loosen the set screws in both wheels. Place a level length wise against the front tooth edge of the blade and adjust the wheels in or out on the shaft until the blade is level. When done tighten the set screws.

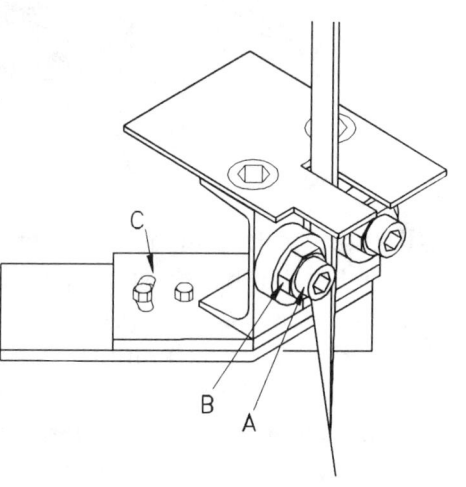

**Figure 142 Adjusting the guide rollers**

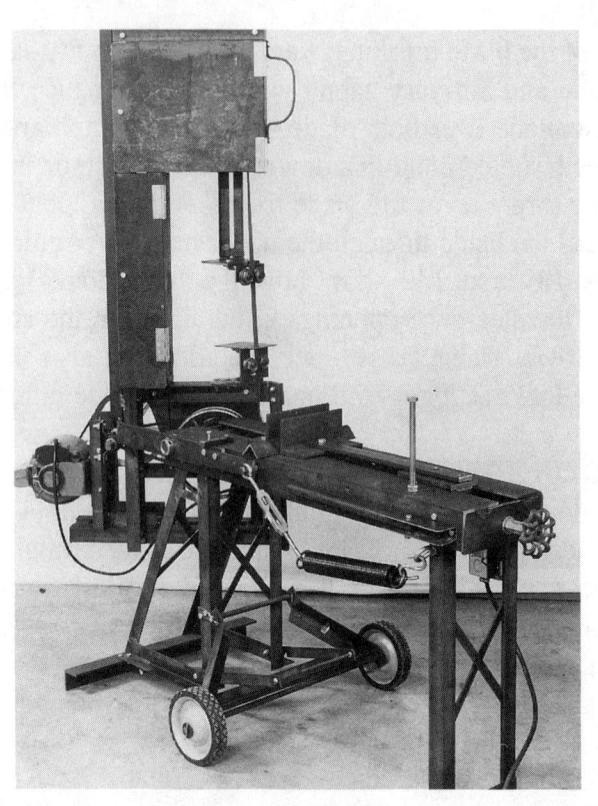

**Figure 143**

All three rollers in both the upper and lower guide roller assemblies can be adjusted by loosening the 3/8 x 1 cap screw that holds the eccentric guide bolt in place. (See item A in fig. 142). Place a wrench on the eccentric guide bolt. (See item B in fig. 142). Adjust the side rollers one way or the other by turning the eccentric guide bolt. The rollers are correctly positioned when the blade barely touches both rollers and it remains straight as it passes through the rollers.

The purpose of the rear roller in each assembly is to support the back of the blade. It is correctly adjusted when it just barely touches the back of the blade when the saw is not being used.

The purpose of the roller guide assemblies is to hold the blade perpendicular to the work. To adjust the lower guide assembly loosen the bolt labeled item "C" in fig. 142. To adjust the upper roller assembly loosen the bolt that holds the assembly to the adjustable arm. See fig. 113 for the location of the bolt.

There probably will be slight differences in angle measurements and differences in the location of the blade wheels that will occur during the construction of the saw. Because of this, the mounting location of the blade guide assemblies may be a little off. This is not a serious problem. If it happens, move the mounting location of the guide assemblies forward or backward as required and redrill the mounting holes.

**Figure 144**

When the blade guides have been adjusted, tighten the blade tension. Don't tighten the blade too tight. The correct adjustment is just beyond the point where the blade no longer slips on the wheels when cutting.

Finally adjust the tilt of the idler wheel. The tilt adjustment makes the blade track properly on the idler wheel. In other words the proper tilt of the wheel is what keeps the blade from coming off the wheel during operation.

The tilt is adjusted by tightening or loosening the adjustment bolts shown in fig. 141. The proper adjustment is at that point when the blade tracks properly on the wheel.

**SETTING THE VISE UP FOR MITER CUTS:** If you want to make miter cuts with the saw it is a simple matter to make the stationary clamp jaw adjustable by substituting the bolt on the left side of the jaw with a 3/8 drop pin.

Set the desired angle by placing an adjustable protractor on the side of the saw table at the cut angle desired. Pull the drop pin and swing the stationary jaw over to the new angle. Mark the spot on the saw table that coincides with the hole in the stationary jaw. Drill a 3/8" hole in the saw table at the marked spot. Reinsert the drop pin securing the stationary jaw at the new angle.

**CUTTING PROBLEMS AND CAUSES:** All saws will be slightly different and will require different adjustments. It takes quite a bit of patience to adjust the blade wheels and guide rollers so that the blade will cut straight. But the biggest problem that you will encounter is the saw blade slipping off the blade wheels. Remember that when you adjust one area, other areas may also require adjustment. The problems I encountered and their possible solutions are listed below.

## SAW BLADE WILL NOT STAY ON BLADE WHEEL:

**(1).** The most likely cause of this problem is that the vertical frame is putting too much weight on the work. To solve the problem adjust the feed pressure control spring. There should be just enough weight on the work to make the cut. Be careful though because insufficient feed pressure can cause premature blade dulling. Watch the cutting action, proper feed is when the chips are curled without being burned.

**(2).** Adjust the tilt on the idler wheel.

**(3).** You may need to change the tilt of the blade wheel by increasing or decreasing the size of the shim under the outer drive shaft pillow block bearing.

**(4).** The guide rollers may be gripping the blade too tight.

**(5).** The guide rollers may be out of round causing them to grab the blade too tight at certain points.

**(6).** Insufficient blade tension.

**(7).** The upper adjustable guide roller assembly could be too far from the work piece.

## BLADE AND TEETH BREAKAGE:

**Caution:** *Do not* rest the blade on the work before the motor is started. This would cause the blade damage. *Do not* drop the blade onto the work. This would cause the blade to break. Begin the cut slow and easy.

**(1).** The blade is too coarse. A minimum of two teeth should always be in contact with the work.

**(2).** Excessive blade tension

**(3).** Guide rollers not adjusted properly

**(4).** Guide roller assemblies are not holding the blade straight.

**CONCLUSION:** Congratulations, you now have a horizontal/vertical metal cutting bandsaw. I hope that you have enjoyed

enjoyed the project as much as we have.

The most important thing to keep in mind as you use your saw is <u>safety</u>. A machine that cuts metal can cut fingers too. There are moving parts, belts, and exposed pulleys on the machine that can cause injury, so keep the little kids away.

As we built the saw we made an effort to keep the costs down yet still produce a working machine. The surprising result was a heavy duty bandsaw capable of doing the work of the more expensive commercial saws. Even so improvements can be made and you are encouraged to make them.

Probably the first line of action should be to paint the saw to protect it from rusting. I believe the frame of the saw is heavy enough to justify the addition of a worm gear drive. Another improvement could be the addition of ball bearing guide rollers. Maybe add a coolant pump and catch pan. These are just a few of the ideas that come to mind. And I am sure there are many other ideas you'll think of as you proceed with the project. Don't be discouraged by the size of the project. Just dig in and enjoy. Remember, when you're through you can throw the hacksaw away.